The Long-Ra...
Guide to Extreme Accuracy

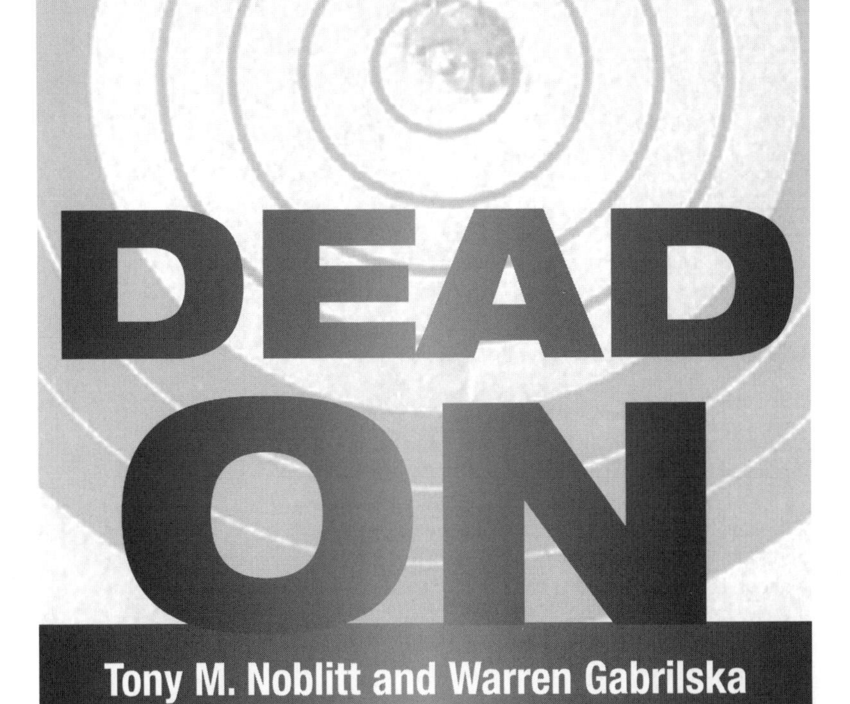

DEAD ON

Tony M. Noblitt and Warren Gabrilska

PALADIN PRESS • BOULDER, COLORADO

Dead On: The Long-Range Marksman's Guide to Extreme Accuracy
by Tony M. Noblitt and Warren Gabrilska

ISBN 0-87364-997-4
Printed in the United States of America

Published by Paladin Press, a division of
Paladin Enterprises, Inc., P.O. Box 1307,
Boulder, Colorado 80306, USA.
(303) 443-7250

Direct inquiries and/or orders to the above address.

Table of Contents

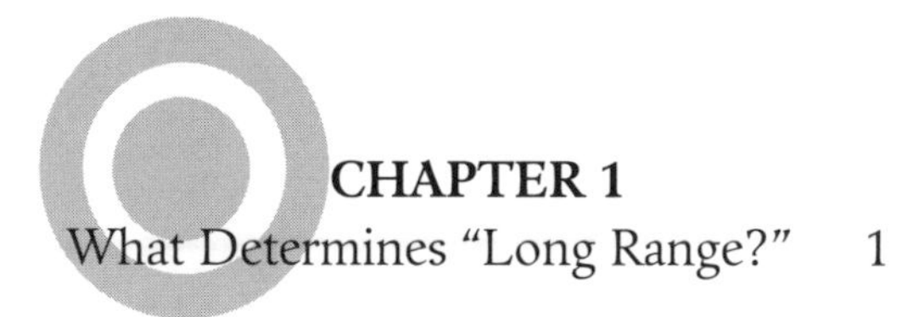

Hats off to my shooting mentors: John Alexander, Stanley Newlin, and Fred Norton.

—Tony

The American rifleman is a peculiar individual. Although his sport is highly competitive, he has always been eager to give to all others full and complete information, holding back no secrets. Perhaps he realizes that in the last analysis he may have to stand shoulder to shoulder with his brother rifleman, in defense of his home, his liberty, and his nation.

—Townsend Whelen
"The Ultimate in Rifle Precision"
1949 Yearbook of the Bench Rest Shooters Association

Chapter 1

What Determines "Long Range?"

To answer this question, we must first consider two factors: target size as it pertains to bullet trajectory and the capabilities of the marksman and his equipment. For example, let's say a boy with his .22-caliber rimfire rifle has a target the size of a small bird. The range is 100 yards. Most shooters would say that the target is out of range. However, if the target was a standing groundhog, no problem! So why is the bird out of range and the groundhog not?

The .22 Long Rifle cartridge sighted in at 50 yards drops approximately 5 inches at 100 yards. The bird, being 2 to 3 inches tall, would be missed by the path of the bullet because at 100 yards it would pass approximately 3 inches below the bird. On the other hand, the groundhog, being approximately 15 inches tall, would still be well within range and would be hit about 5 inches low of point of aim. So, with this simple example we see that the small bird would be considered a long-range shot because a hit would require the boy to hold his aim over the target by about 3 inches. With the groundhog this holdover would be unnecessary and would therefore not be considered long range.

Another factor influencing what is considered long range is wind deflection. The in-flight bullet is deflected by the

The authors practicing what they preach.

effects of wind. If this dispersion becomes greater than the size of the target, it becomes a long-range target because sight corrections are necessary to produce a first-round hit.

So we see that bullet trajectory, target size, and wind deflection, plus the capabilities of the shooter and his equipment, determine what is long range.

AN INTRODUCTION TO LONG-RANGE SHOOTING EQUIPMENT

Having the proper equipment for long-range shooting is necessary to increase the probability of a first-round hit. This does not necessarily mean buying the most expensive equipment available. The equipment must be, above all, reliable and consistent. Used equipment of good quality will perform every bit as well as shiny new things. The following sections will describe the hows and whys of the necessary equipment.

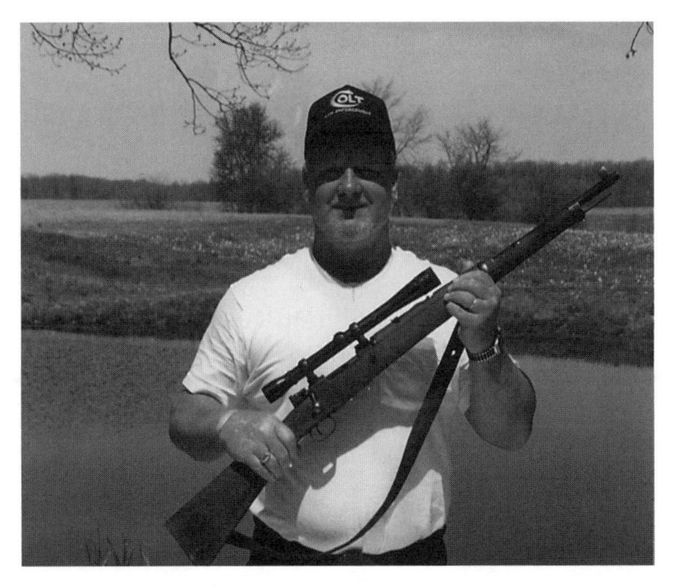

Congressional Medal of Honor recipient Sammy L. Davis with his half-mile capable 1916 Spanish Mauser.

The expendable components, such as bullets, cases, primers, powder, and cleaning materials, are just as important as the rifle, scope, and reloading tools used.

An example of well-used workable equipment is this old 1916 Spanish Mauser in .308 Winchester that we set up. The trigger was tuned to a good two-stage pull that breaks cleanly at about 4 pounds. An older Weaver K8 rifle scope was installed using Burris Signature Series rings. After some load development, the rifle can now deliver a first-round hit on a 2-minute-of-angle (MOA) target out to 800 yards, provided the shooter does his job. There is less than $250 in the rifle and scope. The only new components used on this gun were the scope rings and base. Is the rifle a long-range bench-rest gun? No. Can this rifle be made to hit a 2-MOA target at half a mile? Yes. Better equipment combined with experience can make it easier to connect at long range, but it is not necessary to mortgage the farm to build a rifle system that gets the job done.

The following information about equipment will help you make good decisions about where to spend your money and time to get the best long-range results.

CARTRIDGES

In this book we are going to look at cartridges, bullets, rifles, and equipment with the idea of 1,000 yards being long range.

There are many high-power rifle cartridges capable of 1,000-yard accuracy. A very short list would be the 6mm Remington, .308 Winchester, .30-06 Springfield, 7mm Remington Magnum, .300 Winchester Magnum, and so on. The criteria that determine whether a modern, high-velocity cartridge is suited for 1,000-yard shooting are as follows:

Long-range cartridges. L-R: the .22 Voere caseless, .223 Remington with low-drag bullet, 7mm Remington Magnum, .308 Winchester, .30-06 Springfield, .300 Weatherby Magnum, and 8mm Remington Magnum.

1. The cartridge should be able to keep a bullet of adequate weight above the speed of sound out to 1,000 yards. The accuracy of some bullets is adversely affected when the bullet's speed drops below the speed of sound. This deceleration can have a destabilizing effect on bullets and can result in diminished accuracy. This speed at sea level is about 1,100 feet per second (fps).
2. The cartridge should allow a bullet to arrive at its target with energy adequate to fulfill its mission. An arbitrary number of 500 or 1,000 foot-pounds of energy remaining at the target can be used as a point of reference. A .357 Magnum generates about 500 foot-pounds of energy at the muzzle and a .44 Magnum about 1,000 foot-pounds. A hunter is obligated to deliver enough energy to the game being harvested to

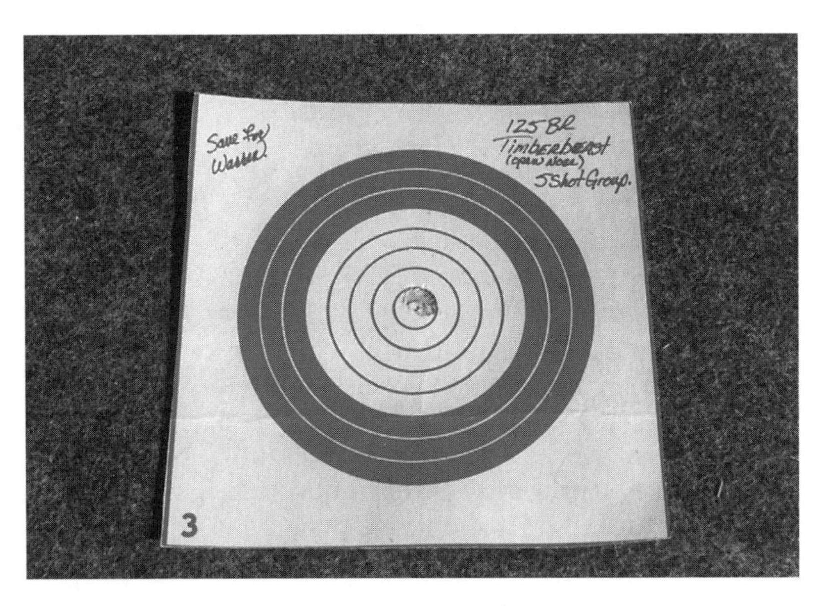

A tight 100-yard group fired by a bench-rest shooter.

humanely dispatch it with one round. If hunting is your activity, the power of the cartridge determines your maximum range.

3. The cartridge must have enough inherent accuracy to shoot 1-MOA groups. Most modern high-power cartridges have this ability. This is mostly the function of the rifle, shooter, and quality of the ammunition.

Below is a list of some common long-range cartridges and their remaining energy at 1,000 yards.

Cartridge	Bullet (grains)	Muzzle Velocity (fps)	Velocity at 1,000 yards (fps)	Energy at 1,000 yards (foot-pounds)
.22-250 Rem.	55	3,700	977	116
.243 Win.	100	2,900	1,159	298
.25-06 Rem.	117	2,900	1,082	304
.270 Win.	150	2,800	1,200	479
7mm Rem. Mag.	168	2,900	1,589	941
.308 Win.	168	2,700	1,190	528
.30-06 Spfd.	180	2,700	1,328	705
.300 Win. Mag.	180	2,900	1,452	842
8mm Rem. Mag.	220	2,900	1,500	1,114
.375 H&H Mag.	300	2,600	1,329	1,176

Those cartridges listed that have a velocity of less than 1,100 fps remaining at 1,000 yards and/or have less than 500 foot-pounds of kinetic energy left at that range will have a maximum range of less than 1,000 yards. It is also important to remember that in the case of hunting, the kinetic energy figures are merely a convenient reference for citing bullet energy. It does not translate directly into killing power or knockdown power. There are many variables that control bullet effectiveness at target range, such as the type of target and bullet construction, which are outside the scope of this book.

BULLETS AND LOW-DRAG TRENDS

Bullets

The bullet is the final factor of the complete rifle system. There are many myths and misunderstandings about bullets and bullet flight at long range. In this discussion on bullets, we will be interested only in flight characteristics, without concern for expansion or penetration qualities.

There are several basic parts to a bullet.

The Base

The base of the bullet is the full-diameter bottom of the bullet. It is one of the most critical areas of the bullet for accuracy. The gas seal or pressure ring area of the bullet must be even and perfectly square to the axis of the bullet. Any variation

At left, the standard 180-grain Hornady hunting bullet as compared with a custom 200-grain low-drag target bullet at right.

or unevenness in the base of the bullet will result in an uneven exit of gasses around the bullet when it clears the muzzle. This results in instability and loss of accuracy. Most bench-rest shooters use flat-based bullets for their 100- and 200-yard competitions, because the perfect exit of gases behind the flat, square base is optimal for accuracy. Boattail bullets have a tapered base, which decreases the area of low pressure or vacuum behind the bullet as it travels through the air. This feature allows the bullet to have less air resistance during flight and will slow the bullet less rapidly than a flat-based bullet of equal diameter, weight, and point configuration. Where boattail bullets come into their own, however, is past 400 yards, where the benefits of reduced air resistance decrease the flight time of the bullet in contrast to its flat-based counterpart, making range estimation and windage adjustments less critical. These factors all add up in making first-shot hits more likely. A third base type, called a rebated boattail, has the features of both a flat-based bullet and standard boattail. In theory, this base design improves the bullet's accuracy potential over that of a standard boattail at the closer range, while still retaining velocity at longer range better than a flat-based bullet. These bullets are available from Lapua of Finland and from a number of custom bullet makers in the United States.

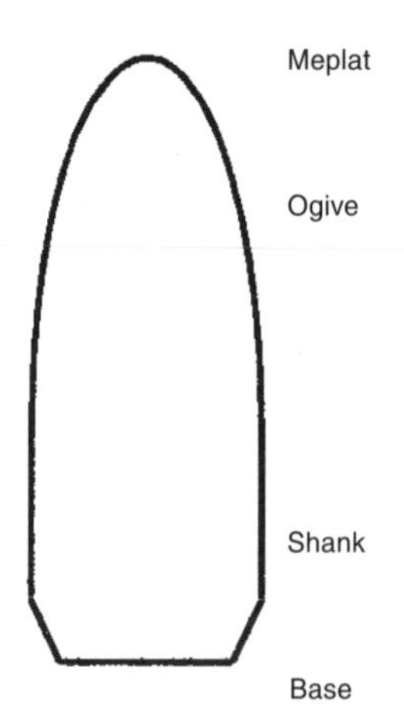

Parts of a bullet.

The Shank

The shank of the bullet is the cylindrical portion of the bullet at its widest part. This is the area of the bullet that is engaged by the rifling. Typically, the greater the length of this area, the more accurate the bullet is. Low drag or very pointed bullets are sometimes a trade-off between shank length and ballistic efficiency. Bullets that sacrifice a long, pointed nose for more bearing surface typically are not aerodynamic enough to perform at long range, and bullets that sacrifice bearing surface for aerodynamic efficiency may give up some accuracy. Most commercially made bullets have a good balance between point shape and bearing surface for use in most situations.

The Ogive

Pronounced *oh-jive*, this word describes the shape of the bullet's point ahead of the shank. This shape is the major factor in air resistance. A blunt, rounded, or squared-off point will cause the bullet to rapidly lose velocity as it tries to push a path through the air. The longer and more pointed the ogive is, the less the bullet is affected by air resistance and the less it will drop across a given distance in comparison with a blunter bullet started at the same velocity.

The Meplat

The meplat of the bullet is the very tip of the bullet. It can be a hollowpoint, a lead tip, or now even a plastic tip as in the Nosler Ballistic Tip or the Hornady V-Max. The size or diameter of the meplat is the main concern; the larger the diameter of the very tip of the bullet, the more air resistance the bullet has and the faster it will slow down. Bullets with very defined points typically perform better at longer ranges than blunter bullets.

Bullets chosen for long-range work should have the highest ballistic coefficient possible and should be dimensionally consistent. The higher the ballistic coefficient, the better the retained velocity. Bullets that have a high ballistic coefficient are typically long and pointed. Most long-range bullets also have a boattail to further reduce drag. The shooter must choose a bullet that will stay supersonic from the chosen cartridge at 1,000 yards.

The other criteria for selection is that the bullet and your particular rifle must like each other. It is not unusual for a rifle to shoot one type of bullet better than another. The only way to determine this is to experiment with different bullets and loads until the best combination is found. The relationship of bullet and rifling twist rate is also very important. The higher the ratio of bullet length to bullet diameter, the faster the rifling twist rate must be to stabilize the bullet. Simply said, longer bullets need faster twist rates.

CUSTOM BULLETS AND TRENDS IN LONG-RANGE BULLET DESIGN

Custom-made bullets are available for many purposes, and there are many small custom bullet manufacturers around the country. Some of these makers specialize in long-range low-drag bullets. The current trend in long-range bullet design is the ultra-low-drag (ULD) bullet. A ULD or very- low-drag bullet is typically a long, pointed bullet with a boattail. These bullets usually require a very rapid rifling twist to stabilize them because of their extreme length. The major advantage of low-drag bullets is their transonic performance. This means they have the ability to stay supersonic longer than standard bullets because of their very efficient shape. The disadvantages of the low-drag bullets are their extreme length and the necessity of rapid rifling twists to stabilize them.

One of the most dramatic examples of the advantages of low-drag bullets is their use in the .223 Remington cartridge. Rifles with twist rates of 1 in 7 to 1 in 8.5 are winning high-

The standard .223 ball round compared with the .223 long-range cartridge loaded with an 80-grain bullet seated to touch the rifling.

power rifle matches, even at 1,000 yards. This is made possible through the use of 75- to 80-grain low-drag bullets. A 1-in-7 twist AR-15 with a free-floated barrel and low-drag bullets is capable of sub-2-MOA groups at 1,000 yards if the wind conditions aren't too extreme. This development turned the "Mattel gun" into a viable long-range rifle.

Some custom bullet makers also have the flexibility to make special bullets tailored to the individual needs of the shooter. If you have a particular design in mind that is not readily available, there is probably a custom maker around who will fulfill your needs. Custom bullets are usually extremely precise because they are made one at a time by hand with a great deal of care. They can be made in special shapes, diameters, and weights. Also, custom makers have the ability to customize the terminal performance of the bullet by making hard or soft cores and prefragmented cores and partitions, and offering many other options as well. Some of the makers specializing in long-range bullets are Berger, JLK, Breise, and TBP. Sierra is also leading the way among production manufacturers in the manufacture of special low-drag bullets.

RELOADING

Reloading your own ammunition is the only way to maximize the performance of your rifle. The first step is to purchase one of the many reloading manuals from bullet manufacturers such as Sierra, Hornady, Speer, or Nosler and study it thoroughly. Basic reloading techniques are covered extensively in many other publications, but we will mention some points relative to long-range shooting here.

The first and most important thing is *safety*. Dangerous pressures can kill. A constant diet of maximum loads will wear out your equipment and possibly your body. It is never a good idea to run loads at the ragged edge of safety. There are always things that can occur outside of your control that can push chamber pressures over the edge. High temperatures, a fouled bore, or a long case can cause a pressure spike that will take your max load and turn it into a bomb. It is best to settle on a load that gives the performance needed with easy extraction and reliability in all conditions. That extra 50 fps is not worth a powered disassembly of your rifle. A rifle with the bolt stuck shut because of a hot round is nothing more than an expensive, heavy, awkward club.

In our 42 years of combined reloading experience, we have found that full-length resizing seems to be best. Strictly neck-sizing generally runs into a lot of hard-chambering rounds. A full-length resizing die adjusted to give easy bolt closing will help maintain trouble-free rifle operation. Nevertheless, we have had some success with Lee Collet dies in some applications. If the cases are going to be fired in the

The reloading bench with presses, scale, powder measure, and numerous other gadgets.

same rifle that they came out of, the Collet die works very well. It is necessary to check the overall length of the case for stretching, and it doesn't hurt to check the resized empties to see whether the bolt will close on them before reloading. Reliability and ease of operation are so very important. It is hard enough to estimate range and wind correctly without having the added distraction of hard-chambering ammunition. Tight-fitting neck-sized cases do give a slight increase in accuracy for bench rest competitions, but are usually not worth the trouble for most long-range shooting. Using tight cases creates a gain in accuracy smaller than the possibility of sighting error and other variables affecting a shot at long range and should be reserved for only the most demanding bench-rest competitions where the aggravation may be worth the very small incremental gain in accuracy.

The key to accuracy is consistency. If all the variables are the same, the rifle will shoot in the same place, but there are

A Sinclair flash-hole-deburring tool.

many variables. It is very important to control those variables that are in our power. High-quality reloading is a good place to start. Cases should be all of one brand and preferably all from the same lot. A simple way to reduce variation in cases is to weigh them. Cases not within 3 to 5 grains of each other should be separated into individual lots. Trim all the cases to the same length. An additional step that can add some consistency and slightly reduce group size is to deburr the primer flash hole from the inside. When the flash hole is punched into the case, it pushes up a substantial burr inside the case. This can cause inconsistent ignition of the powder from case to case. Removing the burr makes ignition that much more consistent. Flash-hole-deburring tools are available from Sinclair International.

Another important point to consider in long-range accuracy reloading is seating depth. Bullets should be seated so that the forward part of the shank is touching or nearly

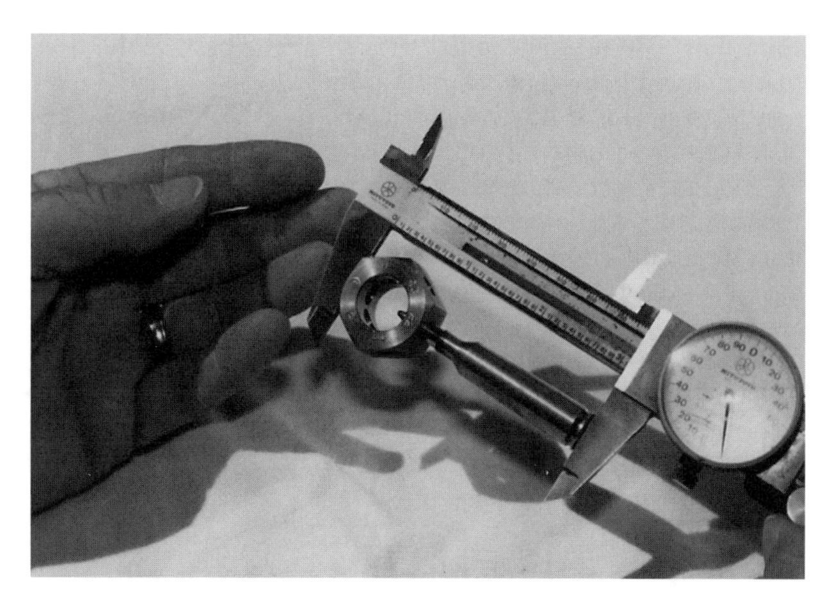

The Sinclair bullet comparitor.

touching the rifling. Magazine length may not allow a bullet to be seated sufficiently close to the rifling. This is especially true with low-drag bullets with extremely long ogives. At this point you must decide whether the repeating function of the rifle is more desirable than the potential accuracy gain of seating the bullets out to the rifling.

One important point to consider about bullet seating depth is how to measure it. The actual length you are concerned with is the distance from the base of the case to the start of the bullet ogive. The overall length of the round only indicates whether the round will fit in the magazine. Bullets, especially ones with lead tips, vary considerably in length. The variation in length is usually confined to the length of the ogive. The dimension from the base of the bullet to the start of the ogive is the dimension that must be consistent, and usually is. Checking the overall length of loaded ammunition will not guarantee that the shank is a consistent distance from the rifling. Measuring the distance from the base of the case to the start of the ogive can be done with a Sinclair bullet comparitor. This is the real dimension to measure for consistent bullet-to-rifling fit.

The new reloading manuals on the market contain a wealth of good information. The more you learn about reloading and shooting, the easier it is to understand why things work or don't work in the field. Knowledge is power.

Consistency, consistency, consistency. Make every aspect of your reloading consistent and you will have consistent results. With close attention to your ammunition, cleaning of the bore, and practice from the bench, 1/2-MOA accuracy is obtainable.

Did we mention consistency?

RIFLES

For cost, reliability, and accuracy, bolt-action rifles are the first choice for long-range shooting. The U.S. Marine Corps has always thought along this line, and recently the U.S. Army followed suit. Both the Marines (1967) and the Army (1988) adopted the Model 700 Remington bolt-action rifle for sniper use. There are many types of bolt-action rifles very well suited for long-range shooting, such as the Winchester Model 70, Remington Model 700, Steyer SSG, and Savage 112, to name just a few that can be bought almost ready to go for long-range work.

Rifles to be used for long-range shooting should have very stiff and heavy barrels that are "free-floated" and triggers with light, crisp pulls.

Single-Shot Bolt-Action Rifles

One type of bolt-action rifle that is made expressly for long-range shooting is the Paramount or Swing-action rifle. (Swing refers to the inventor, not the function of the action.)

These are single-shot rifles made out of a very heavy, rigid tubular receiver. The ejection port is as small as possible to maintain maximum rigidity in the action. The bolt lift is very short and heavy, and the firing pin spring is very heavy as well to give the fastest lock time possible. These rifles can be found mainly in long-range high-power rifle matches and are shot at 600 and 1,000 yards, and they turn in some impressive performances. These rifles are a good choice if a single-shot will fill your needs.

Semiautomatic Long-Range Rifles

There are some semiautomatic rifles that are accurate enough for long-range shooting. The military M14/M1A .308 Winchester (7.62mm) was the U.S. Army's standard sniper rifle and has been used in 600- and 1,000-yard competition for many years with good results. These rifles need special bedding and tuning to perform at long range.

A surprising newcomer to the field of long-range shooting is the AR-15 rifle. This rifle, with a free-floated barrel, good trigger, fast rifling twist, and heavy low-drag bullets, performs quite well at 600 and even 1,000 yards if conditions are not too extreme (very gusty winds and so on). The AR-15 has an accuracy advantage over the M1A in that there is no gas piston system attached to the barrel to affect accuracy. Properly set-up AR-15s are capable of sub-MOA groups at long range, although admittedly the bullet does not deliver a tremendous amount of energy at extended ranges.

Heckler & Koch makes a .308 Winchester semiauto based on the HK-91 action that is designed as a police countersniper rifle. It is called the PSG1 and is as accurate as most bolt-actions. The only drawback to this rifle is its high cost (between $8,000 and $10,000).

Also, Walther makes a semiauto countersniper rifle in .300 Winchester Magnum that performs admirably for its very specialized task.

SCOPES

To some, a rifle scope is a mystery, but it's simply a precision alignment tool that also magnifies the sight picture. By gathering additional light and magnifying the target, the shooter sees target definition many times greater than with the naked eye.

There are a multitude of fixed-power and variable-power scopes available. Variable-power scopes are more versatile, but fixed-power scopes are less complicated. There are also many reticle designs. Some are simple cross hairs, whereas others are called duplex, post, inverted-post, range-finding, mil dot, and multicircle reticles. All of these designs have varying purposes and provide a precision aiming point.

The main advantage of the telescopic sight is the single sighting plane, which allows you to focus on one plane—the target.

For long-range shooting, maximum target illumination is highly desirable. Therefore, purchase the largest scope objective you can afford (40mm to 50mm).

All modern scopes have internal adjustments and should be of 1/4- or 1/8-minute graduations. For shooting to 1,000

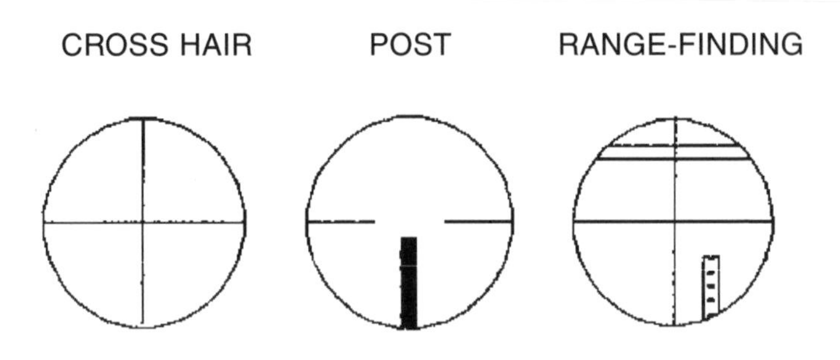

A Weaver V16 target scope mounted on a Remington Model 700 chambered in .308 Winchester.

yards, the scope must have a minimum of 60 minutes of internal elevation adjustment. This is needed to compensate for bullet trajectory drop over a distance of 1,000 yards. Most modern high-power cartridges that are capable of this range and remain supersonic will drop (from a 100-yard zero) approximately 50 MOA or less. Magnification should be no less than 10X. However, this could be a handicap in some competitive shooting matches because of greater aiming error than that of scopes with higher magnification. With a 20X or more scope with fine cross hairs, aiming error is less than a quarter-minute (2.5 inches) at 1,000 yards. We prefer fixed-power scopes of no more than 15X because at times mirage can be overwhelming at higher magnifications.

The scope must have adjustment knobs, which are large finger-turnable knobs marked with adjustment graduations. These are needed for the many adjustments of elevation and windage while shooting in changing conditions. They should be zeroable in that when the rifle is sighted in at 100 yards

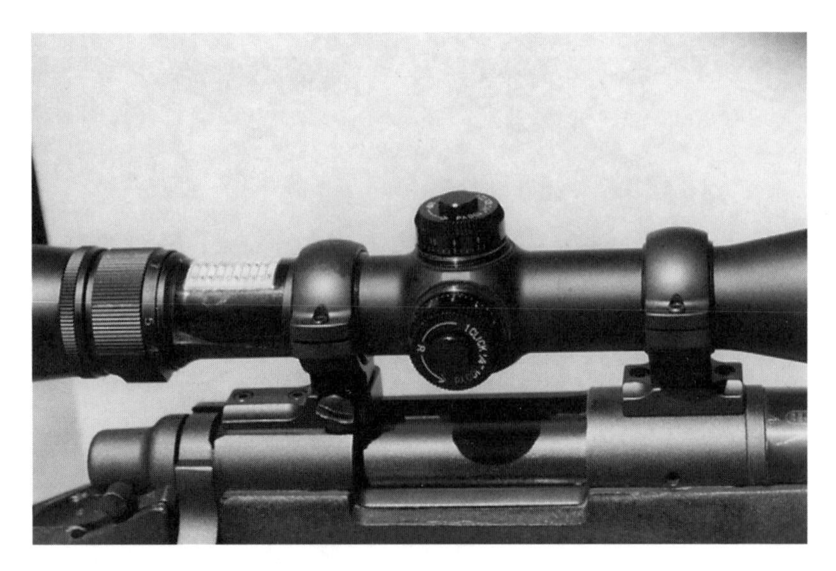

Adjustment knobs on a Weaver V16.

and all the adjustments are made, the knob graduations can be reset to zero, which sets the scope adjustment graduations at a 100-yard zero. Without this feature a rifle scope is only good for shooting at point-blank range.

Another feature needed is an adjustable objective bell. This is necessary to keep the scope parallax free at the range of the target (parallax is the apparent change in the position of an object, in this case the scope reticle, resulting from a change in the position from which it is viewed). In other words, when looking through the scope in a rock-solid position with cross hairs fixed on a target, if you move your eye up and down or side to side and the cross hairs move, this will cause a change in the point of impact. This means that if there is parallax present and you don't look through the scope exactly the same way on each shot, the point of impact will change, which will keep you from obtaining a correct zero. This is a real problem for scopes without this adjustment that are only set parallax free at 100 yards.

METAL SIGHTS

Metal or "iron" sights are a forgotten tool for long-range shooting, except for high-power rifle competitors. Iron sights have frequently shot their way to 1-MOA groups (10 inches) at 1,000 yards during National Match events. However, iron sights do have some disadvantages in comparison with scope sights for all-around long-range shooting. The first disadvantage is the absence of magnification—what you can't see you can't hit. The second disadvantage is that the sights and target are on three different planes, which makes focusing more difficult.

All long-range target shooters use peep sights. Most of them use an aperture front sight, except for service rifle shooters. Aperture front sights are the best thing going for shooting round targets against a contrasting background,

Redfield target sight with 1/4-minute adjustments.

A Redfield target sight mounted on a modified 1903 Springfield.

although for field shooting they make target acquisition difficult. A better aperture for field work is a plain post front-sight insert. This arrangement allows for better visibility through the front-sight tube. The major problem with post front sights is that the shooter has to visualize a horizontal line going straight across the rear aperture, and he must bring the front post exactly up to that line. If the shooter is not disciplined enough to do this, substantial vertical stringing will occur.

Target sight adjustments work just like a target scope. Most target sights are set up with 1/4-minute adjustments. The industry standard for target sights are Redfield Palma and International sights, which are very well made and never fog. Adjustable apertures are available for changing light conditions. Other very high-quality target sights are available from Anschutz, Paramount, and Mo's.

The U.S. Army uses backup target sights on its M24

An aperture front sight with spirit level.

A post front sight is best for targets of irregular shape and for general field shooting.

sniper rifle, which can be a lifesaver if a scope gets damaged. If a first-round hit is your primary goal, a scope sight is a better tool, but knowing how to use high quality iron sights can get the job done in a pinch. Don't ignore them; they work.

BIPODS

Bipods are two-legged devices that attach to the rifle and function as a portable shooting rest. A bipod does not appreciably increase the weight or portability of the rifle and can be a good field aid in making long-range shots. The bipod must not be attached to the barrel of the rifle because it will cause a shift in the point of impact. The stud for mounting a bipod should be set up to level the rifle to reduce the effects of canting while shooting.

Bipods are available from Harris, Inc. and the B-Square Company. Good bipods are adjustable for canting and

The Harris bipod folded and deployed.

The correct starting position for using a sling. The loop is around the upper arm, and the hand goes over the sling and under the rifle.

height, which makes them very versatile for shooting over obstructions.

SLINGS

The use of a rifle sling for shooting is an art largely ignored by most shooters. High-power and smallbore competitors are probably the only shooting groups who realize the benefits derived from a properly used rifle sling, which can give a shooter a solid shooting platform when a bipod is too low or a rest is unavailable.

The target sling being used in the sitting position. Note that the left hand does not grip the rifle tightly.

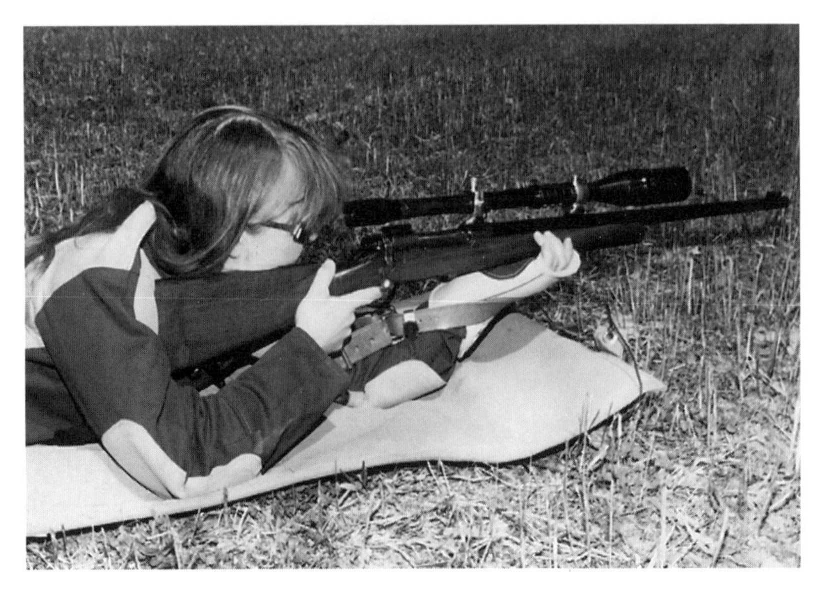

The target sling being used in the prone position, which is the steadiest of all unsupported positions.

Sling Types

Leather Military Slings

Military slings offer many advantages to the shooter. When properly adjusted, the sling provides a comfortable carrying strap as well as a quick shooting support when used in the "hasty" mode and a precision rifle support when used as a loop sling.

It does take some study to properly assemble and adjust these slings. One of the disadvantages of this sling is that it is slightly narrow for use as a loop sling without a shooting jacket with a padded pulse pad (where the loop fits around the shooter's upper arm). Without the pulse pad, the sling will pinch and rapidly cut off circulation to your supporting hand.

A standard military-style leather sling.

Military Web Slings

Web slings are military utility slings made from cotton webbing and metal clips. They are very inexpensive but quite functional, quickly adjustable for carrying, and make a very functional loop sling for target work. These slings are as narrow as the standard military leather slings and will pinch and cut off circulation just as fast. One small detraction of this sling is that the metal buckles rattle unless taped.

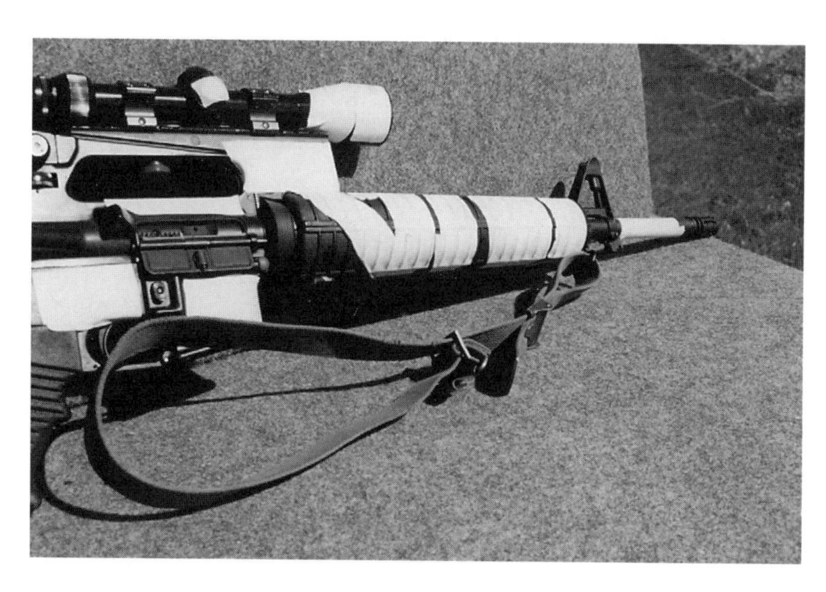

A military web sling on a snow camo AR-15.

Target Slings

Target slings come in several styles, but they generally attach to the rifle with a quick-release buckle. The quick release attaches to the rifle in a rail let into the bottom of the stock. The sling attachment point is adjustable anywhere along this rail, allowing a perfect sling position in most any shooting situation.

A target cuff sling showing the loop around the upper arm.

Target slings usually have a wide cuff where the loop goes around the upper arm. This reduces pinching and circulation loss, although these problems can never be completely eliminated even if proper sling technique is used.

The first rule of using target slings is *tighten it up!* If the sling isn't super tight, it isn't giving you optimal support.

The "CW" or "Ching" Sling

The CW sling was rediscovered by Jeff Cooper and employs an old technique of attaching a sling at the front of the stock and again directly ahead of the trigger guard. This looks unconventional but is quite versatile and uncomplicated with a little practice. A reversed cobra-style sling works very well, as does a simple carry strap mounted in this manner.

Proper Sling Technique

To properly use a target loop sling, the left arm (right arm if you are left-handed) is put through the loop of the sling and

A "CW" sling in use on a No. 4 Mk. 1 Enfield. The sling is attached at the fore-end and in front of the trigger guard.

the loop is tightened above the left biceps. The hand and arm then go over the sling, down, under, and around the sling, and then under the rifle. The V formed by the thumb and forefinger of the left hand butt firmly into the junction of the sling and rifle. The left hand should not grip the fore-end of the rifle and the fingers should be relaxed. If you are shooting in the prone position, your left elbow must be directly under the rifle and the sling tension must be sufficient to hold the rifle in place without the aid of muscles.

Adjusting the length and position of the sling on the rifle will fit the system to your body. A shooting glove on the left hand will make the target sling much more comfortable.

The shooter must take care that when it is in position, the rifle is not tipped or canted left or right, which will cause changes in point of impact. Care must also be taken to ensure that the fore-end of the rifle is kept rigid enough to avoid deflection when heavy sling pressure is applied. It is possible with rifles that do not have free-floated barrels to pull the point of impact off with sling pressure. (Unfloated standard-weight AR-15s can be pulled off a full 12 minutes by sling pressure.) A rigid forearm and a free-floated barrel will eliminate this problem.

RELATED EQUIPMENT

Equipment that is necessary for testing, practice, and competitive or field shooting is as important as the rifle itself. This is a list of equipment you'll need.

1. Solid shooting bench
2. Mechanical rifle rest with front and rear sandbags
3. Stock-mounted bipod and rifle slings

A shooting bench with some of the equipment you'll need.

A shooting mat properly set up.

4. Shooting mat
5. Spotting scope of 20X or greater
6. Wind flags
7. Bore-sighting tool (collimator)
8. Two one-piece cleaning rods, one jag, and one brush
9. Paper towels (we prefer Bounty®) for use as cleaning patches
10. Bore guide
11. Hoppes #9 cleaning solvent
12. Sweets 7.62 solvent or other copper-removing solution
13. Pocket calculator
14. Pocket wind meter

Chapter 2

Setting Up the Rifle

BULLET PATH AND LINE OF SIGHT

In setting up the long-range rifle, it is important to have an understanding of the factors that affect bullet flight and bullet path or trajectory, the primary two of which are gravity and air resistance. The effects of gravity are constant for any bullet, but a bullet's air resistance is affected by a great many things, such as speed, humidity, elevation, and bullet shape.

An easy way to visualize bullet path is to observe water coming out of a garden hose. Assume the hose nozzle is spraying a high-pressure solid stream. The stream behaves exactly like a bullet in flight but on a smaller scale. If the nozzle is held parallel to the ground, the water immediately begins a curved path to the ground, never getting any higher than the nozzle. If the nozzle is angled upward, the path is in the shape of a bullet's trajectory.

Let's say that you are in your garden with the hose. Your neighbor's dog is standing in a row of tomato plants 10 feet away. You can spray a straight stream of water to hit the dog because you are so close that elevation isn't necessary because the speed of the water gets the water to the target faster than gravity can pull it down. Now the dog moves off to the edge of the garden 50 feet away. He shakes off the effects of your close-range blast and begins digging a hole in your wife's rose bed. You aim the nozzle straight at the dog and let fly. The water lands short of the target and the dog continues throwing dirt. You angle the hose up and let fly again. The water makes a parabolic arc, soaks the dog, and saves the rest of the roses.

You go back to watering the garden, standing on the side of the garden with your back to the wind, watering the row of pepper plants at the far side of the plot. You have the nozzle angled upward so that the water lands right on the pepper plant directly downwind. As you water the peppers along the row, you turn more into the wind with each plant. For the water to hit the plants upwind you have to angle the nozzle farther into the wind and make elevation angle adjustments.

The garden hose is an accurate analogy to bullet flight and is one of the best ways to visualize what actually occurs.

Let's examine bullet path in several scenarios.

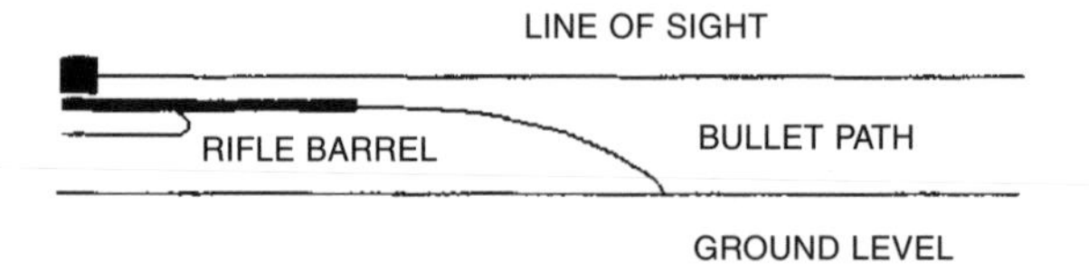

Rifle Fired with the Barrel Parallel to the Ground

Once a bullet is fired from a rifle in this position, it immediately begins to drop. If there is no backstop and the ground is perfectly level, a bullet fired from any rifle will hit the ground at the same time as a bullet dropped from bore height. The force of gravity works straight down with the same force and effect on everything, regardless of its forward motion. (Note: For those nitpickers out there, a fired bullet develops a slight amount of lift in flight and will strike the ground some microseconds after the dropped bullet. There is no practical difference. However, the distance the bullet traveled before hitting the ground can vary tremendously.)

Let's look at the variables that can affect the distance the bullet will travel in this scenario.

Velocity

The faster a bullet is launched, the farther it will travel before hitting the ground. (Note: Even though the velocity is higher, the time of flight for any bullet in this scenario is exactly equal because gravity is a constant.)

Bullet Shape

The only force that slows a bullet in this scenario is air resistance, which is directly related to the bullet's shape and weight. A longer, more pointed bullet will travel farther in the same amount of time than a shorter, blunter bullet. A boattail on a bullet will also allow a bullet to travel farther in the same flight time than a flat-based bullet because of the reduced area of vacuum at the base of the bullet. The number that quantifies this property is called ballistic coefficient, which is a number that represents a bullet's ability to resist deceleration due to air resistance. The higher the number, the lower the bullet's air resistance, which means it will travel farther during its given flight time.

Rifle Fired With the Barrel Elevated Above the Horizon

This scenario demonstrates real-world bullet flight.

Let's again assume that the line of sight of this rifle is parallel to the ground. As the bullet leaves the muzzle it immediately starts to drop, but because the barrel is elevated, the bullet crosses the line of sight at some point on its ascending path. The bullet's path then peaks and starts to fall. Crossing the line of sight on its descending path is typically the zero range of the rifle. As the distance from the muzzle increases, the rate of drop increases, thus requiring the rear sight or

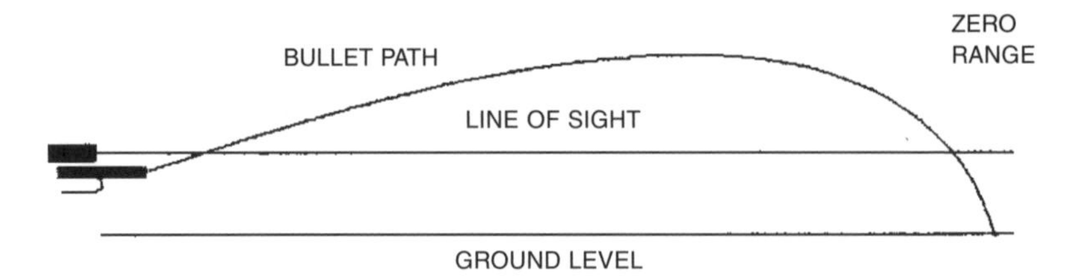

scope reticle to be higher. Because the line of sight is a constant, this lowers the breach of the barrel and elevates the muzzle to maintain zero. The farther the bullet goes, the faster it drops. This is due to air resistance and gravity working on the bullet. As the bullet slows down because of air resistance, the distance covered per unit of time becomes less and less, which allows gravity to pull the bullet down more and more per unit of distance traveled.

As in the first scenario, a longer, more pointed bullet shape reduces the effects of air resistance and will extend the distance the bullet travels per unit of time.

WHAT IS MOA?

Understanding MOA is very important in setting up a rifle and scope combination.

All scope adjustments for elevation and windage are made in MOA. There are several methods of measuring angles, the most common and familiar of which (in the United States) is the DMS system (degrees, minutes, seconds). This system divides a circle into 360 degrees, such as on a compass. Each degree is further divided into 60 minutes, which are further divided into seconds (60 seconds per minute). Rifle shooters need only be aware of minutes of degrees, seconds being too small to have any appreciable value for this application. (MOA is also the standard measurement for scope or target sight adjustments.) Most scope adjustments are in 1/4-minute increments. Four clicks on most scopes will move the point of impact 1 MOA at any range (1/ 60th of 1 degree).

The actual size of a MOA increases as distance increases. This can be easily visualized as a long, skinny triangle with the narrow pointed end resting perfectly on the firing pin of your rifle. The bottom leg of the triangle goes straight out the rifle barrel perfectly parallel to the ground all the way to a target 100 yards away. The top leg of the triangle also starts at the firing pin of your rifle. If the angle of dispersion between the two lines is 1 MOA at 100 yards, the distance between the two lines is almost exactly 1 inch. Now visualize the same triangle with the bottom leg extending out to a target 200 yards away. The distance between the two lines is now almost exactly 2 inches at 200 yards. With the target 1,000 yards away, the distance between the two lines is now 10 inches. The result of all this geometry is that if your sights are changed 1 MOA, your point of impact will move 1 inch at 100 yards, 2 inches at 200 yards, 6.5 inches at 650 yards, and 10 inches at 1,000 yards.

COMPASS

All scope and sight adjustments in this book will be in MOA.

MOA DISPERSION

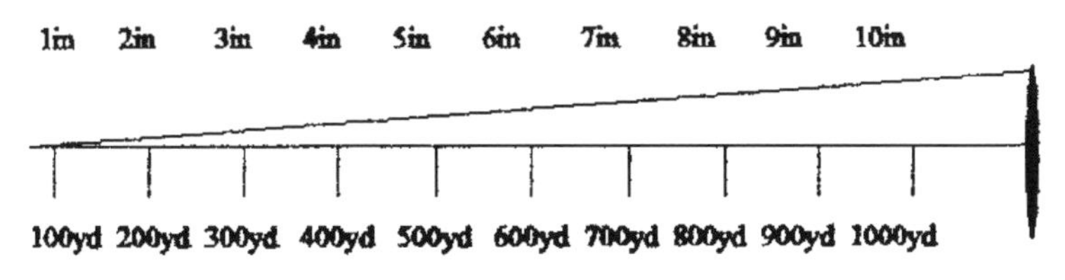

POINT-OF-AIM/POINT-OF-IMPACT SHOOTING VERSUS POINT-BLANK SHOOTING

Before mounting the scope, we must define the difference between point-of-aim/point-of-impact shooting and point-blank shooting.

In point-blank shooting, the scope is generally aligned with the bore of the rifle and sighted in at a particular range that allows the shooter to aim "dead on" for a target of known size. This is only effective within a specific distance. For instance, if you sight in your .30-06 Springfield deer rifle 3 inches high at 100 yards, you will have a point-blank range on a deer (10 inches diameter is vital) from the muzzle to about 300 yards. What we are addressing is point-of-aim/point-of-impact shooting where the rifle is zeroed for 100 yards and exact adjustments are used to cause hits beyond point-blank range. If point-blank shooting is desired with a rifle set up for point of aim/point of impact, all that is necessary is the proper scope elevation adjustment for a specified range.

Setting up a rifle and scope for point-of-aim/point-of-impact shooting will allow you to easily use both shooting techniques as situations require. Versatility and flexibility allow you to be more effective.

RIFLE WEIGHT

Today the long-range shooter has a smorgasbord of long-range rifles that can be purchased almost ready to go, right out of the box. But what is "ready to go?"

First, comfort and ease of shooting must be established. How much should the rifle's total weight be to oppose the recoil of a specific round? It must be understood that these gun weights are heavy for one purpose: long-range shooting out to 1,000 yards. We have had exceptional results with a Remington Model 700 Varmint Special in .308 Winchester

A McArthur muzzle brake installed on an AR-15.

while shooting off of a Harris bipod, often printing 7-inch groups at 1,000 yards (under ideal conditions). But this gun was sometimes difficult to shoot because of recoil. In choosing a rifle, decide on the cartridges to be used and caliber first, then make sure it is heavy enough for the recoil factor.

Based on the weight and recoil of the Marine Corps M40A1 sniper rifle at 14.5 pounds firing a 168-grain bullet at 2,700 fps and generating about 2,700 foot-pounds of kinetic energy, we came up with a factor of 1 pound of rifle weight for every 200 foot-pounds of bullet energy at the muzzle.

This factor is only valid for medium-bore cartridges and only gives a comparison to the military rifle. For instance, the .270 Winchester with a 150-grain bullet at 2,800 fps and 2,600 foot-pounds of energy would have an optimal weight of 13 pounds (2,600 foot-pounds ÷ 200 = 13). The .308 Winchester with a 168-grain bullet at 2,800 fps and 2,924 foot-pounds of energy would have an optimal weight of 14.5 pounds. The .300 Winchester Magnum with a 180-grain bullet at 3,000 fps and 3,597 foot-pounds of energy would have an optimal weight of 18 pounds.

This is merely a guideline for determining a certain comfort level for recoil as it relates to ease of shooting. Certainly an 18-pound .300 Winchester Magnum has a downside in the weight and portability department. Combine this weight with your commonsense factor to come up with a weight that is right for you.

These factors do not take into account the use of muzzle brakes. These devices thread onto the muzzle and use the escaping powder gases to reduce recoil. A properly designed and installed brake can reduce the felt recoil by 50 percent or more. This can allow you to reduce the weight of the rifle while maintaining shooting ease and comfort. The downside of brakes is noise; most muzzle brakes greatly increase the muzzle blast of a rifle. Always use ear protection when shooting, especially when the rifle you are shooting has a muzzle brake.

FLOATING THE BARREL AND STOCK MATERIAL

You must make sure that the barrel is free-floated. This means that the barrel is free from touching the stock forearm all the way back to the receiver. This allows the barrel to whip and vibrate freely when fired and will react in the same way shot after shot. Remember that consistency means accuracy. To check for barrel-to-stock clearance, run a thick strip of paper between the barrel and forearm. It should slide freely with no dragging. If there is any tightness, the clearance must be opened up.

Stock material is important, too. Wood was the standard from the beginning, but because it is greatly affected by adverse weather changes, which can cause it to warp and swell, it's not the best choice today.

Synthetic stocks are here to stay because they are more durable and stable than wood. But beware of cheap, plastic polymer stocks that are flimsy and soft or spongy in the forearm, which makes them very difficult to shoot with. They also warp rapidly in the hot sun and put pressure on the barrel, thus causing the point of impact to shift. Avoid these cheap stocks at all costs. High-quality synthetic stocks made from

A dollar bill slid easily between the barrel and the barrel channel demonstrates no contact.

fiberglass, Kevlar, or graphite are rigid and durable. These stocks are manufactured by Bell & Carlson, McMillan, and H-S Precision, among others.

The area of the stock into which the action fits is called the bedding area. To bed the action means to apply liquid aluminum, steel, or fiberglass to ensure a perfect mating of the stock to the action. This further increases rigidity, which aids accuracy. Instructions on how this is done come with bedding kits available from Brownells, Inc.

H-S Precision and Bell & Carlson rifle stocks are the exception to this bedding process in that they come with solid aluminum bedding blocks molded into the stock. Bell & Carlson's New Technology stocks have a frame or chassis molded into the stock. This new design strengthens the pistol grip area with a tube of extremely light aluminum that connects to the bedding block. From the bedding block for-

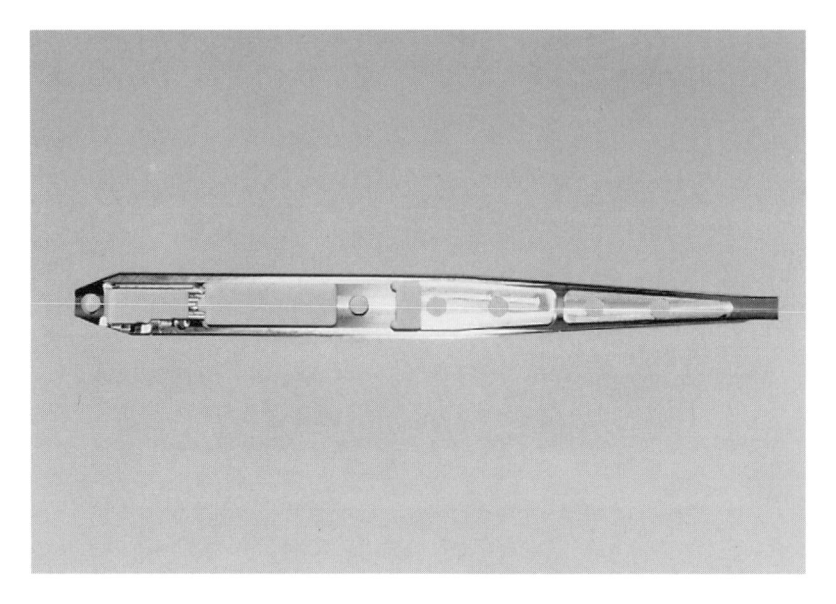

A magnesium chassis ready for molding into a Bell & Carlson synthetic stock.

ward, two solid frame rails extend and tie together at the swivel stud. This provides a ridged mounting point for the bipod that is connected directly to the action. All this stiffens the action, thus enhancing accuracy. These truly are drop-in, ready-to-go rifle stocks.

THE TRIGGER

First and foremost, *if you don't know how it operates, don't mess with it.*

Trigger pulls should be set with 3 to 4 pounds of pull with absolutely no creep before or after release. It if needs adjustment, go to a qualified gunsmith and have this work performed. Lighter pulls can be had, but safety must be your first concern, so think twice before going less than 3 pounds.

Aftermarket triggers are available from Timney, Canjar, and others. If the trigger in your rifle is unsatisfactory, have a better

A Timney trigger.

one installed. Trigger release and lock time are critical to accuracy. The quicker the ignition and bullet exit, the less chance there is of gun movement throwing the shot off its mark.

MOUNTING THE RIFLE SCOPE

Scope Bases

First on the list are scope mounting bases. There are various types, but we are only going to discuss and use the universal rotary dovetail bases. Because of their windage adjustability, they solve the problem of initial windage adjustment. This way the preadjusted scope can be zeroed with the bore for windage and still be in the center of its adjustment travel, while only using offset ring inserts for elevation alignments.

One- or two-piece bases? One-piece rotary dovetail bases should be chosen strictly for target rifles. They add weight and also stiffen the action. Two-piece bases allow for clear-

One- and two-piece scope bases.

ance between bases, scope, and the top of the action for ease of carrying. This clearance allows placing of the thumb under the scope and grasping of the rifle at a point of balance.

When mounting the bases, oil them lightly and wipe them free of excessive oil. Do the same with the top of the action. Use Loctite 242 Threadlocker on the screws to prevent them from working loose from recoil. Tighten them, but don't break them off.

Rings and Inserts

Next are the mounting rings. There is only one type that we are going to discuss because of its considerable alignment advantages. This is the Posi-Align ring system from Burris, Inc. Burris's outer steel ring combines with synthetic inserts that come in .000, .005, .010, and optional .020-inch offsets. These rings are definitely a better mousetrap because they allow for precision alignment while mounting the scope.

Burris Posi-Align scope rings and inserts.

Bore-Sighting Tools

Bore-sighting tools are also important. There are two types that we are aware of: the grid type, which consists of a grid in which the squares are either 2 or 4 minutes (inch) with a total of 20- to 80-minutes spread (available from Redfield and Bushnell), and the crosshair type, which is a cross hair with 2-minute graduations and a total of 100-minutes spread. The latter is the type we prefer because the scope can be run through its total adjustment range. This

A Bushnell bore-sighting tool.

tool was available from Bushnell as the True Scope, but unfortunately is no longer in production, although you might be able to find one by checking *Shotgun News* or other such sources.

Grid type bore-sighting tool.

Scope mounting can be accomplished by the average rifleman using common tools. You will need a gun vise or other means of resting the rifle firmly, a magnetic level, and the appropriate screwdrivers and Allen wrenches.

The procedure for setting up a scope on a rifle is as follows:

1. Set the rifle solidly in a vise or on sandbags. Level the rifle by using a magnetic level across the top of the scope bases.

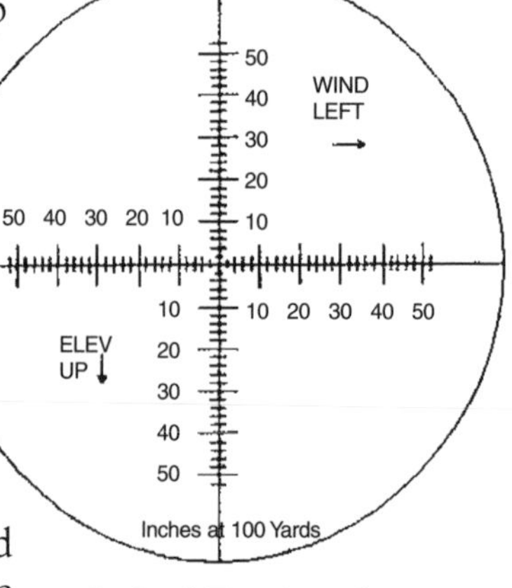

Bushnell True Scope bore-sighting tool

2. The front scope ring should be turned into the base and aligned parallel with the face of the action. Mount the rear ring and center it in the windage adjustment screws at the center of the rear base. Now remove the top half of the rings and put the bottom half of the .000-inch inserts into the bottom half of the rings.

3. Preadjust the rifle scope windage to center of travel by running the adjustment all the way to the left, then run the

A rifle set on sandbags with a level across the top of the scope bases.

adjustment all the way to the right while counting the number of revolutions of the adjusting knob. Return left half of the total number of revolutions. This is the center-of-windage adjustment for this scope. Zero the adjuster graduations to this setting by loosening the screw holding the adjuster turret and turning it until it is at zero. Tighten the screw. Now run the elevation adjuster to the very bottom (down) of its travel. Come up one-half revolution of the adjusting knob and zero the adjuster graduation setting. This half-revolution allows enough down adjustment for sight-in at 100 yards. The scope is now preadjusted for mounting. Once zeroed, if the shooter loses track of his settings he can easily return to his 100-yard zero by running the elevation adjuster all the way down and coming back up to the nearest zero.

4. Set the preadjusted scope in the lower ring halves. Slide the scope back and forth until the proper eye relief is achieved. Eye relief should be set slightly forward so as to cause the neck to crane slightly forward to get the proper eye relief. This so-called preloading of the shooter's neck will allow shooting under free recoil conditions without the scope's hitting the shooter in the eye. While looking through the scope, turn the scope until the horizontal cross hair is parallel with the top of the bases.

A bore-sighting tool inserted in the muzzle.

5. Insert the bore-sighting tool with the proper size stud into the muzzle of the rifle.

   Look through the scope and turn the bore-sighting tool until the horizontal grid or cross hair in the tool is parallel (level) with the horizontal cross hair in the scope. Put the top halves of the .000-inch inserts into the top halves of the rings. Attach the top halves of the rings to the bottom halves and snug down evenly.

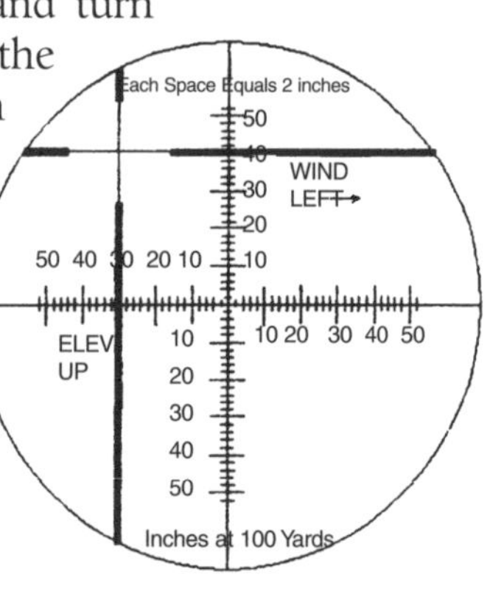

Use scope base windage adjustment to center vertical cross hair.

6. Check the alignment of the vertical cross hair in the scope with the vertical cross hair in the tool. Use the windage adjustment screws in the rear

scope base to align these two cross hairs. Once these are aligned, tighten the screws firmly and use Loctite to keep them from working loose.

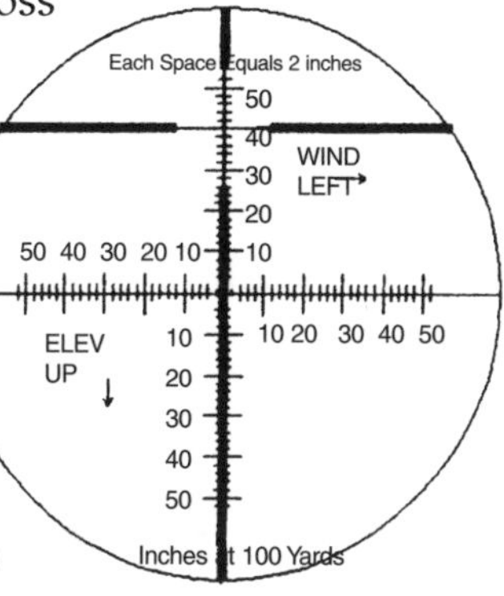

Vertical cross hair centered.

7. If the horizontal cross hair of the scope is above the main horizontal cross hair or grid line of the sighting tool, the rear of the scope is too low. Using the instructions that came with your sighting tool, determine how many minutes of difference there is between the cross hair of the rifle scope and the center of the sighting tool. The best way to describe what must be done now is by example.

   If the horizontal cross hair of the scope is 40 MOA above the center of the bore-sighting tool, remove the top halves of the scope rings, remove the scope, and replace the .000-inch insert in the bottom of the rear ring with a +.020-inch insert. Then replace the .000-inch insert in the bottom of the front ring with a -.020-inch insert. Lay the scope in the bottom half of the rings, adjust the scope for eye relief, and align the horizontal crosshair with the sighting tool. Now replace the .000-inch insert in the top rear ring half with a -.020-inch insert and replace the .000-inch insert in the top front ring half with a +.020-inch insert. Reinstall the

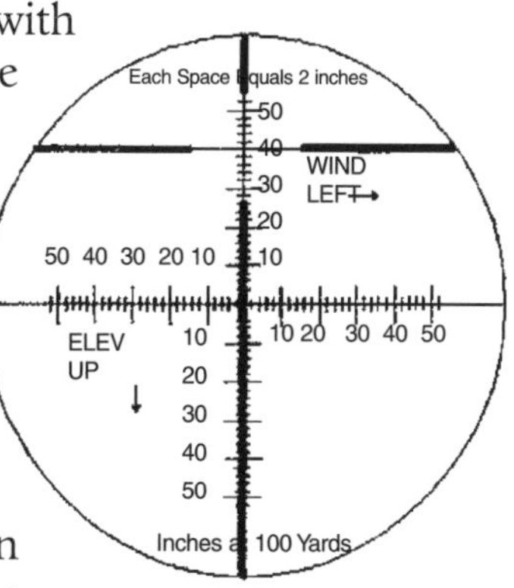

Tip scope 40 MOA to center.

top halves of the rings and snug down evenly.

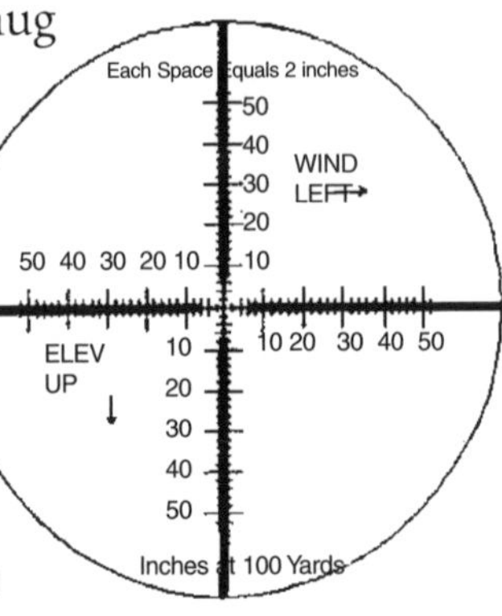

Cross hairs centered.

The scope's horizontal cross hairs should now be aligned with the horizontal cross hair of the bore-sighting tool because the scope has been tipped 40 MOA by the use of the ofset Burris rings. This allows for maximum elevation adjustment of up to 50 minutes. The scope's cross hair should now coincide with the center of the bore-sighting tool. If additional shimming is necessary, brass or stainless-steel shim stock can be used under the rear ring insert (.001-inch is equal to 1 MOA).

8. Now the scope can be checked for adjustment run-out. If there is any run-out as the cross hairs are adjusted up from the bottom to the top and left to right, it should be noted. More than 1 MOA of run-out is unacceptable and the scope should be removed and repaired or replaced.

Now that the scope is mounted, there will be 40 to 50 minutes of elevation adjustment, 25 minutes of left windage, and 25 minutes of right windage adjustment. The rifle is now ready to be sighted in for zero at 100 yards.

External-Adjustment Scopes

External-adjustment scopes such as the Lyman, Fecker, and Unertl can be handled in much the same manner as modern scopes. These scopes are tubes with centrally mounted cross hairs that are set in special mounts with micrometer adjustments built into the mount. When the adjuster is moved, the whole tube of the scope is physically moved in the mounts to cause a change in point of impact. This results in a system that is very reliable. The value of each "click" is determined by the spacing between the front and rear scope bases. The standard spacing of 7.2 inches between front and rear blocks will deliver 1/4-minute adjustments per click. Blocks spaced farther apart will deliver smaller values per click, and blocks closer together than 7.2 inches will deliver values larger than 1/4 minute.

There are two styles of external-adjustment scope mount-

A Unertl external-adjustment 15X Ultra-Varmint scope mounted on a 1917 Enfield target rifle.

A Posa scope base for a Unertl scope. This style holds up better under recoil.

ing blocks: the standard target blocks and the Unertl Posa blocks. The target style is more common, but the Posa blocks deliver a more solid mount for rifles with heavier recoil.

These scopes can be set up in a manner similar to conventional internal-adjustment scopes. Instead of using the Posi-Align rings to position the scope for maximum elevation range, different scope block heights can be used to angle the scope mounts so that the 100-yard zero setting is near the bottom of the elevation adjustment.

Scope blocks are available in many heights to accommodate nearly any situation and are available from Unertl and several other sources. Even though these scopes look like antiques, they are very functional long-range tools. They are also one of the best ways to understand the relationship between line of sight, sight adjustments, and angle of bore. If the rifle is zeroed at 100 yards with an external-adjustment scope and you want to adjust the rifle to hit a target at a dis-

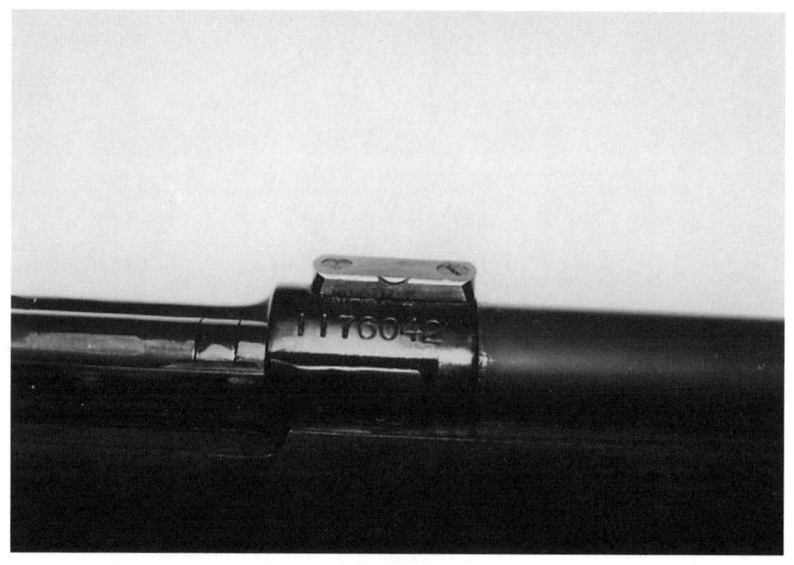

A target-style scope base. Note the shallow notch.

tance that requires 34 minutes of elevation, you would turn the elevation adjuster 136 1/4-minute clicks up. This physically moves the tube of the scope 34/1,000ths of an inch up in the rear mount. This in effect angles the rifle muzzle 34 minutes of a degree up from its 100-yard position when it is aimed at the distant target. This is truly how sight adjustments cause point-of-impact changes because the line of sight through the scope is constant. The movement of the scope mount actually moves the rifle in relation to the constant line of sight.

Chapter 3

Zeroing

SHOOTING FROM THE BENCH

Shooting from the bench is the oldest form of experimenting with and testing rifles. But there are things you have to do to get the most out of shooting from the bench.

The bench must be level and solid with no wobble or wiggle. A rest must be used, such as a sandbag or bipod, but mechanical shooting rests are best because they are adjustable for height—and some for windage as well. Some popular brands are Bald Eagle, Hart, and Wichita. Front and rear sandbags along with rests are available through many shooting supply outlets.

Set your target at exactly 100 yards. (Don't just step it off; measure it with a steel tape. You must be very precise. Precision and consistency result in accuracy.) With this accomplished, set wind flags at 50 and 100 yards. They are simple to construct using 1/2-inch PVC pipe. Cut two pieces of pipe about 5 feet long. Attach to each a stiff wire that a ribbon can be loosely tied to, which will allow the ribbon to twist in the wind. Shove them in the ground and you are all set.

Set the fore-end of the rifle on the front sandbag rest.

Shooting from a bench rest.

Move it about until the bag conforms to the shape of the fore-end. Place the rear bag under the buttstock. Sitting down, your body should be at a 45-degree angle to the line of fire.

Looking through the scope, adjust the rear bag back and forth until the cross hairs settle on the target. (The rest may need to be adjusted for height so that a comfortable sitting position can be attained.) Lightly grasp the pistol grip, holding the trigger finger away from the trigger. Use your left hand to squeeze the "ears" of the rear bag to adjust it for elevation aiming errors.

Your shoulder should not be pressed against the buttpad, but the buttpad should be lightly felt. (Note: This technique is for heavy target or varmint guns. Lighter guns of heavy caliber may require a tighter hold, thus being more difficult to shoot accurately.) This is also where correct eye relief is a must, or a cut or shiner is the result. Placing the ice bag on the shiner should be very light, just as placing the cheek

The proper position of the left hand on the rear sandbag.

should be very light on the cheek rest or comb of the stock. Too much pressure will result in a shot going left. Too much right-hand pressure will result in the shot going right. (This would be reversed for left-handed shooters.)

When placing the trigger finger, use only the part of the finger between the last joint and the tip. As the rifle goes off, the last thing seen should be the cross hairs on the target. If there is any horizontal movement, the shot will move off in that direction. After the shot is fired, the rifle must be slid forward on the bags or returned to battery. This must be done exactly to the same position shot after shot.

Practice is the only way to perfect your technique. Practice firing five-shot groups and working with your ammunition until you get 1-inch groups or better (1/2-inch preferably). These groups should be measured from center of bullet hole to center of bullet hole. Now adjust the scope for point of impact at 100 yards. Once the gun is shooting consistently to point of impact at 100 yards, you may reposition the adjustment graduation knobs to zero. The rifle is now zeroed and set up for long-range shooting.

WHY IS ZERO AT 100 YARDS SO CRITICAL?

Why is zero at 100 yards so critical? Because .001-inch movement of the crosshairs at the reticle is equal to 1 inch or 1 MOA. This equals 5 inches at 500 yards and 10 inches at 1,000 yards. Any error in the 100-yard zero is magnified as the range increases. Therefore, the zero at 100 yards is very critical.

To help check your scope's adjustments and repeatability, you can make up a target that is 18 inches x 48 inches with a 1-inch square as an aiming point. The aiming point should be located at the bottom center of the target. Along the left side of the target, 1-inch graduations should be laid out starting even with the aiming point. Put a center line up the middle of the target, making sure that it is square with the target. When setting the target up, use a level to make sure it is level. Now, with practiced procedures, fire one shot, making sure the cross hairs are not canted but level with the target at the center of the aiming point. (Canting or tilting the rifle will cause aiming errors, and at long ranges these errors will be magnified with MOA dispersion.) The hit should be centrally in the square, which verifies zero. Now adjust up 10 minutes and fire again, verifying a +10-minute elevation.

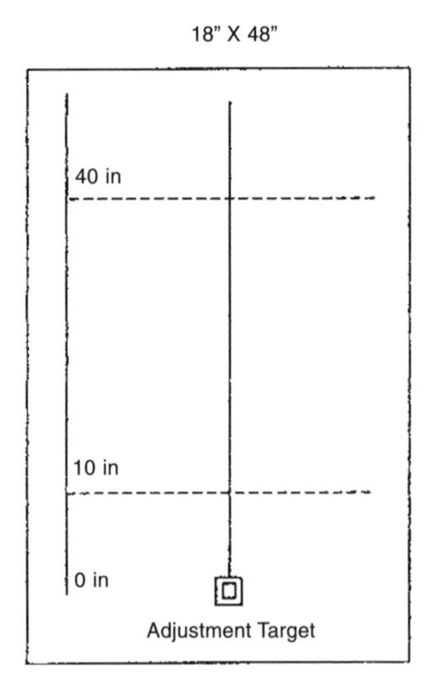

Now adjust up to +40 minutes and shoot to verify a +40-minute zero. Fire a five-shot group to verify, then adjust back down to zero (0.0) and fire again. The hit should be back in the aiming square. All of this verifies that the scope adjusters are working and will return to zero after actual firing and recoil.

HOW TO CONVERT BALLISTIC DATA TO SCOPE ADJUSTMENTS IN MOA

To know what the adjustments for elevation and windage are for your rifle and caliber-cartridge combination, you must consult the ballistic tables in your reloading manual. An excellent example is in the *Sierra Rifle Reloading Manual.* Turn to the ballistic table for the bullet type you are using. Example: .308 Winchester 168-grain HPBT (hollowpoint boattail) match. There will be a chart showing range, energy in foot-pounds, drop in inches, bullet path in inches, zero range, deflection or wind drift in inches, and velocity in fps.

First, you must know the approximate muzzle velocity of your bullet type. Proceed to that velocity reading and look for bullet path with a 100-yard zero (0.0). Make a scope adjustment range card by writing down a range yardage scale. Do this in one column on the left side of the paper.

To the right, start two more columns headed as ELEV. ADJ. and WIND ADJ. 10 mph as shown here.

100		
200		
300		
400		
500		
600		
1,000		

YARDS	ELEV. ADJ.	WIND ADJ. 10 mph
200		
300		
400		

Using a velocity of 2,800 fps, look for the bullet path at 200 yards with a 100-yard zero (-4.5 inches). That is the exact drop of the bullet from line of sight at 200 yards with a 100-yard zero. To zero the scope for 200 yards, divide 4.5 by 2 (2 represents 200 yards). (Note: divide by 4 for 400 yards, 6 for 600 yards, and so on.) You will get an answer of 2.25 minutes. This is the amount of up elevation adjustment needed to zero the scope for 200 yards. Write this figure of +2.25 in the ELEV. ADJ. column across from 200 on your scope adjustment range card. Do these calculations for each corresponding bullet path and range yardage with a 100-yard zero. Round these off to the nearest 1/4-minute. Write each resulting figure under the ELEV. ADJ. column across from the proper range. These figures are MOA scope adjustments needed to zero the rifle from a 100-yard zero to the range that is desired. Your card should now look like this.

YARDS	ELEV. ADJ.	WIND ADJ. 10 mph
100	+0.0	
200	+2.25	
300	+5.25	
400	+9.0	
500	+13.0	
600	+17.75	
1,000	+45.25	

For wind adjustment calculations, go back to the ballistic table and look for the crosswind deflection figures based on 10 miles per hour. At 100 yards this figure is .08 inches. Round off to the nearest 1/4-minute. Write it under the WIND ADJ. column on your range card. Next, look at the 200-yard 10-mph crosswind figure and divide by 2. Your answer is 1.65 minutes. Round this figure off to the nearest 1/4-minute. That is a figure of 1.75 minutes, which you now write under the WIND ADJ. column across from 200 yards. Again, do these calculations for each corresponding 10-mph wind deflection (wind drift) and range. (Note: remember to divide by 3 for 300 yards, 5 for 500 yards, 9 for 900 yards, and so on.) Write each resulting figure under the WIND ADJ. column across from the proper range. These figures are the scope adjustments in MOA for wind drift in a 10-mph crosswind.

Your card should now look like this.

YARDS	ELEV. ADJ.	WIND ADJ. 10 mph
100	+0.0	0.75
200	+2.25	1.75
300	+5.25	2.50
400	+9.0	3.50
500	+13.0	4.75
600	+17.75	6.00
1,000	+45.25	12.00

These figures are rounded off to the nearest 1/4-minute because most scopes adjust in 1/4-minute click adjustments. Most reloading manuals that have ballistic tables only give data out to a range of 500 yards, or in Sierra's case 600 yards, and then skip to 1,000 yards. This is because high-power competitors shoot at 600 and 1,000 yards. For the additional 700-, 800-, and 900-yard bullet path and crosswind data, Sierra offers a ballistic service with a toll-free telephone number that you can call for this information. Or, set up targets and start shooting! The next alternative is a ballistic computer program offered by Sierra (Sierra III). This program is outstanding because the user can plot trajectories out to a maximum range of 2,000 yards. It allows for atmospheric conditions, elevation, sight height, elevation angle, and crosswind direction and speed. If you own a computer, this program is a must.

With a small weather station that gives you temperature, relative humidity, and barometric pressure, preparing for a day of long-range shooting is just a matter of pushing a few buttons. Creating scope adjustment range cards for current conditions is a snap.

THE STANDARD LOAD

Once you have established a bullet, powder, and primer combination, or even a factory ammunition load that consistently shoots 1/2 to 1 MOA, make this your standard load. This gives you a standard baseline of performance from which to make trajectory and atmospheric condition calculations. This baseline is essential for consistent performance and is the basis for which a first-round hit becomes a reality, not a probability. You should always continue a test program in search of a more accurate load. However, refrain from continual load changing while shooting at long range. Sticking with an accurate load provides you with the familiarity that is necessary to predict how the bullet will react in atmospheric conditions that are continually changing. Lots of practice will bring your skill up to the level required to produce a first-round hit. Shooting at targets and observing where your shots are hitting, and then making corrections to get on target, are easily accomplished. But the knowledge necessary to make a first-round hit at extreme range is accomplished by firing many rounds in practice and spending hours patiently observing the surrounding conditions. This observation of conditions must become second nature. We have found ourselves taking note of wind direction and speed when not shooting or even anticipating shooting. This comes from growing up in a hunting environment, which required concentration and attention to detail with patient observations. Without this commitment, the most accurate rifle in the world will make no difference in your ability to produce first-round hits.

MAINTAINING ACCURACY BY CLEANING THE BORE

When shooting rifles, fouling of the bore slowly occurs with each shot fired. As this fouling increases, point of impact will begin to change and accuracy will suffer. Additionally, if this fouling is not removed, barrel wear increases: powder residue builds up, and as a bullet passes down the bore the fit gets tighter and causes metal fouling. The bullet jacket material, generally copper, starts to strip from the bullets, which is very detrimental to accuracy. As copper builds up, it causes rapid metal fouling—and plenty of it, making cleaning much harder.

It is very important to maintain accuracy by keeping the rifle bore clean and free of copper fouling. We have found that cleaning the bore between shot groups is the easiest way to maintain accuracy. When testing loads for accuracy, we generally swab the bore after every five-shot group. First, dry-brush the bore for a few strokes with a bronze brush. Next, run one loose-fitting patch with Hoppe's Bench Rest solvent on it through the bore and then run one or two tight-fitting patches to dry it. This may seem excessive, but if you want to see which load is the best, you have to give them an equal chance.

A patch pushed almost out of the muzzle is easily checked for copper streaks by illuminating the patch.

Normally we clean the bore every 20 to 40 shots, depending on how clean the load is burning and whether we observe any copper fouling. To check for copper, take a dry, clean patch and run it through the barrel until it is 3/8-inch to 1/4-inch from the muzzle. Hold the muzzle up to a light source; the light reflecting off the white patch will light up the bore quite brightly. Any copper strips will be lit up, making them very easy to see.

Incorrect cleaning can do as much damage to the bore as not cleaning it at all. Always clean from the breech and use a bore guide.

A bore guide aligns the cleaning rod and keeps it from wearing on the chamber throat. If possible, clean the bore while the barrel is still hot or warm, or at least as soon as you can after shooting. If the bore is cleaned while still warm, the fouling is much easier to remove.

With the rifle sitting on the bags, remove the bolt. Start out with a loose-fitting patch of Hoppe's and shove it through. Next, use your bronze brush to stroke the bore 10 to 15 times. Now go back to a tighter patch of Hoppe's and shove it through. Use a dry, tight-fitting patch and then go back to a wet one with Hoppe's. Dry the bore out with a couple of fresh patches. This should remove the powder residue. Now run a clean (white), dry, tight-fitting patch to within 3/8-inch to 1/4-inch of the muzzle and check for copper fouling.

Cleaning a rifle from the breech using a bore guide.

Be sure and get the light on it so you can really see it well. To remove the copper, use Sweets 7.62 solvent. Apply this solvent to a loose-fitting patch and run it into the bore. Hold a left-hand finger over the muzzle. Stroke the patch back and forth in the bore; as you do this it will foam slightly. Once it has begun to get foamy, shove it all the way out of the muzzle. Wait 10 to 15 minutes and flush out the bore with a loose-fitting patch of Hoppe's. The patch should be bright blue-green. Shove a tight dry patch through, then another tight wet one. Dry with a couple more fresh patches.

Check for copper and repeat if needed.

(Note: We use Bounty paper towels for cleaning patches. They are very easily torn to adjust for size and work best when folded over double and run through the bore. They work great and are very cheap.)

Chapter 4

Let's Try It At Long Range: Known-Distance Target Shooting

RANGE DESCRIPTION

If you're lucky enough to live in a very rural area and have access to a place to shoot at long range, you are fortunate indeed. One of us has a 1,000-yard range right outside his back door and we shoot off a bench on the patio. This has allowed us a great deal of experience. We don't think we are the very best shots out there, but this experience goes a long way.

We've made some interesting targets that save lots of time and effort. Using 1 1/2-inch exhaust pipe, we built target holders that are capable of holding plywood targets or steel gongs. They are lightweight and very easily moved. The steel gongs for 600 yards are 1/2-inch thick and 12 inches in diameter. (This is 2 MOA in diameter.) For 1,000 yards they are 1/4-inch thick and 20 inches in diameter. They hang on 3/8-inch chain with no welding. (Shock from impact usually destroys welds very quickly.) These steel gongs hold up very well at longer ranges, and the chain will stand hits from hollowpoint or softpoint bullets.

It is very easy to record a hit as the gong swings. At these ranges the bullets leave nice impact marks in the paint that can be seen very easily through the rifle scope or spotting scope at 1,000 yards, provided the mirage isn't bad. We paint them with florescent orange paint. They are repainted after a group has been fired. On close inspection these impact marks are very clear and distinct. The centers of the hits are easily defined, making center-to-center measurement fairly accurate.

Ideally, the range should face north or northeast, which allows better sunlight on the targets. You should have an earthen backstop 10 to 20 feet high. Range descriptions and specifications are available from the National Rifle Association (NRA).

Wind Flags

For long-range shooting, wind flags should be set at 50, 300, 600, 800, and 1,000 yards. We prefer flags to be thin, lightweight, fluorescent orange ribbons. They will move and dance with very light breezes and indicate wind speed and direction indications.

TRACERS, WIND DRIFT, AND TRAJECTORY

Although military tracer ammunition is not noted for its accuracy, it can really shed some light on the effects of wind on a bullet in flight. I have seen times when the wind seemed to be blowing a particular way by observing the flags. When a tracer round was fired, it would first fly as expected for wind drift, suddenly make an unexpected deviation, and then return to its previous trajectory according to the wind deflection as observed by watching the flags. This can be explained by the surrounding terrain features that tend to break up air movement, which cause air movement to be lighter in one area and more concentrated in another. This concentrated air movement or "jet" may be several feet higher than your line of sight and wind flags, and the mid-range trajectory of the bullet could be as high as 12 feet or more above the line of sight. The bullet's path will be affected by this unseen jet of air. (Note: tracer ammunition can be a danger in that it ricochets very easily and could pose a fire hazard. Shoot tracers only where they can be fired safely.)

Shooting just a few tracers while learning how the wind affects bullets in flight can be very educational and fun. Also, the trajectory can be seen all the way to the target. Tracers will not duplicate match load accuracy or trajectories and shouldn't be used to adjust zero for your match loads.

ELEVATION AND WINDAGE ADJUSTMENTS

Let's set up and do some shooting.

For a 600-yard zero, with your rifle prezeroed at 100 yards, check your scope adjustment range card for elevation adjustment at 600 yards. For example, let's say you are shooting a .308 Winchester with a 155-grain Palma bullet at 2,800-fps muzzle velocity. This adjustment calls for +15.0 minutes. (For adjustments, + is up and - is down.) Turn the elevation adjuster one revolution up. (Most scopes have 12 minutes per revolution, but some have 15 minutes.) This will bring you back to zero on the elevation graduations. Add 3 more minutes of up adjustment and this will be +15.0 minutes elevation. This should be zero at 600 yards. Patiently study the wind conditions by observing the wind flags. (This may take 10 to 20 minutes.) Slight winds and breezes generally aren't steady; they seem to blow in patterns, which come and go in intensity. Through study, you can pick the pattern that holds steady for the longest period. This is your shooting "window."

Shooting from the bench, fire a shot and watch for the hit. If you're really on your shooting technique, you will see the impact through the rifle scope. This is where you must know the size of the target. When shooting at our steel gongs, they are 2 MOA or 12 inches in diameter at 600 yards. By seeing the impact, you know how many minutes adjustment are needed to get on target. Watch the wind conditions and fire a second shot in the same wind pattern. (Hopefully, this will be a hit. There will be times in gusty winds that you may have to fire shots in more than one wind pattern. Noting the results will give you an idea of "hold off" or a quick windage adjustment for the wind pattern changes.)

Now let's go to 1,000 yards. Assuming that the scope is still adjusted for 600 yards, it would be at +15 minutes elevation. For example, say you were shooting in a 5-mph crosswind for the current conditions. This has the windage adjustment set at 2.5 minutes right, which means the wind was blowing from the right, causing the bullet to drift left approximately 15 inches. To adjust, the scope was set 2.5 minutes right (15 inches ÷ 6 [600 yards] = 2.5 minutes). Remember, it gets tougher as the range increases. On this day the scope adjustment range card calls for +36.75 minutes elevation from a 100-yard zero. You already have +15 minutes, so turn the adjuster on up to 0 (+24.0 minutes). Turn up one more revolution to 0 again (+36 minutes elevation). Add three more 1/4-minute clicks and you are at +36.75 minutes elevation. If you get lost on the adjustment graduations, turn the adjustment knob all the way down until it stops. Come back up to zero. This is the 100-yard zero. Now you can start over.

Now we need to set the windage adjustment. With the scope already set at 2.5 minutes right for 600 yards, we need to set it for a 5-mph right-to-left crosswind at 1,000 yards. Look at your range card for the WIND ADJ. 10 mph at 1,000 yards block. This figure is 10.25 minutes for a 10-mph crosswind. Divide 10.25 by 2 because a 5-mph wind is only half of a 10-mph wind. The rounded-off figure is 5 minutes. This is the amount of scope adjustment in minutes needed to compensate for a 51-inch wind drift in a 5-mph crosswind at 1,000 yards.

Actual shooting at different ranges and in varying wind conditions is the best practice. Your skill level will increase as you gain experience.

ESTIMATING WIND DIRECTION, SPEED, AND VALUES

Estimating wind direction, speed, and value by reading the wind flags is something that comes with experience. Watching the ribbons move with breezes, you will get a sense of wind speed by how the ribbons hang. As the air moves faster they will begin to stand up, fluttering with the direction of the wind. It's really quite simple to estimate winds from 5 to 15 mph. Hand-held wind meters are available through the Midway Shooters Supply catalog. They measure wind speed from 0 to 60 mph and fit in your pocket.

Horizontal Deflection

Wind value is the angle of the wind and how it influences bullet deflection (drift). Because the wind doesn't always blow as a crosswind but can come from or toward the target at any angle, we use a system of values. Imagine a vast clock with you in the center and the target being at 12 o'clock. Once you have determined wind speed, you need to know its value.

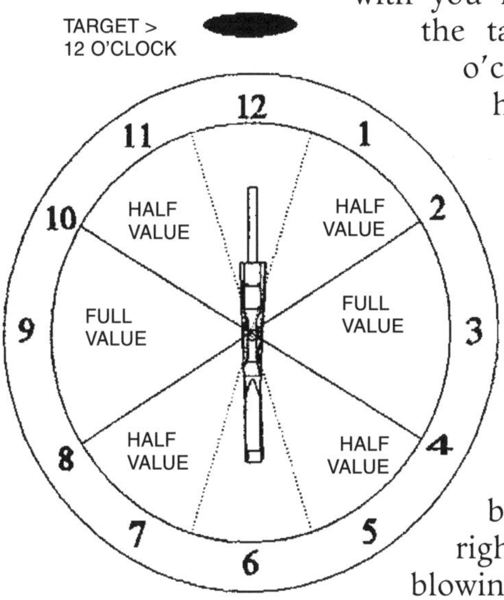

By using the clock as a scale, a tail wind blowing from 5:30 to 6:30 is of no value because it doesn't affect bullet drift left or right. A head wind blowing from 11:30 to

12:30 has no horizontal value. Winds blowing from 10:00 to 11:30, 12:30 to 2:00, 4:00 to 5:30, and 8:00 to 6:30 are half-value winds. Winds blowing from 8:00 to 10:00 and 2:00 to 4:00 are at right angles and have a full value. If the wind is blowing from 1:30 and the wind speed is 15 mph, you would divide your full-value windage adjustment by 2 for a half-value adjustment. To get the 15-mph MOA adjustment from your 10-mph range card reading, multiply by 1.5. Always keep a calculator handy.

Vertical Deflection

Head winds tend to slow the bullet because of added air resistance and the resultant drag. This is why the point of impact is lower. Tail winds cause just the opposite, thus making point of impact higher. This is called vertical deflection and is not as pronounced as horizontal wind deflection. At

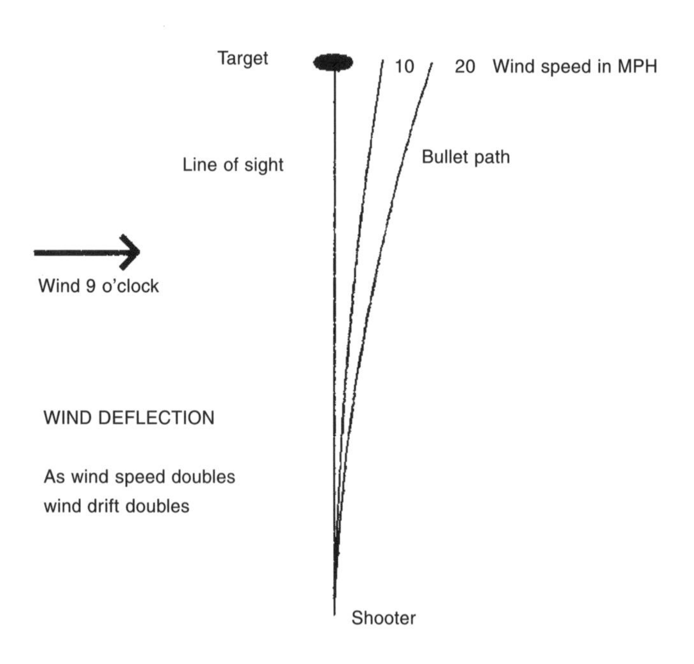

1,000 yards a .30-caliber match bullet will have about a 1/2-minute vertical deflection up with a 10-mph tail wind. With a 10-mph head wind, the deflection will be about 1/2 minute down. A half-value head wind or tail wind will be about 1/4-minute deflection. There isn't any set formula or system to help figure vertical deflection, and most shooters don't even consider it. Sierra Bullets' ballistic computer program gives all the vertical deflections, even with the oblique wind angles. If you want exact figures for all ranges and wind angles, this program is the only way to go.

SHOOTING WITH A SPOTTER

Having a spotter watching with a spotting scope can be of great assistance to the shooter. The spotter doesn't have recoil

The authors. The shooter watches the target while the spotter observes the conditions and bullet impact. The spotter is also responsible for heckling the shooter whenever appropriate.

to contend with and has a clean, undisturbed sight picture. The spotting scope should be at least 20X, but no more than 35X, so that the field of view is large enough to see the bullet trace at mid-range, or at the bullet's highest point above the line of sight, and still be focused on the target. (Bullet trace is the trail of compressed air that is the bullet's shock wave as it passes through the air. A spotter can watch this trace all the way to the target and see where the bullet goes. You don't actually see the bullet, but you can see this trace of compressed air, although there are times when the sunlight is just right so that you can see a bullet in flight because of the reflection of light off the bullet. I've watched .22-250 Remington and .45 ACP bullets all the way to a 100-yard target while shooting with the sun at low angles.)

When the shooter has fired a shot, the spotter watches this trace and then calls out corrections in MOA. The shooter then makes adjustments and is ready to fire with corrected aim. For more on this, we recommend *Reading the Wind and Shooting Techniques* by Jim Owens.

Chapter 5

First-Round Hits

Why are first-round hits important?

The reason varies with your shooting purpose. Hunters require first-round hits because game doesn't stand around to allow sighting shots while you adjust your zero. We in no way condone shots taken at game beyond the limitations of power, accuracy, and conditions. A clean kill is the obligation of all hunters, and if it is not a virtual certainty, then the shot should not be taken. By developing your skills as a long-range marksman, your ability may make longer shots possible. Only you know the limitations of your equipment and yourself. It is irresponsible to exceed those limitations.

Long-range varminters need first-round hits at long range for the same reason that big-game hunters do: varmints don't hang around long after being shot at. An understanding of the principles involved in long-range shooting definitely increases the number of successful shots taken on varmints. Varminting is probably one of the best ways to practice and improve your long-range abilities, because ranges are never the same and conditions must be interpreted correctly to connect. (It's also probably the most fun you can have with your clothes on.)

Military and police snipers must have the ability to make first-round hits. In a military or police situation, not only does your target not hang around after being shot at and missed, he will probably want to return the favor. A military or police sniper's life expectancy can be shortened dramatically if more than one round is fired from any given position. A miss is not only a lost opportunity, but can also be a life-shortening experience. Furthermore, a police countersniper must make a first-round hit to save the lives of the innocent, not to mention the fact that law enforcement personnel are liable for every round fired; the fewer rounds that are fired to accomplish the mission, the less chance there is of incurring property damage or killing or injuring innocent people. First-round hits are essential!

Target shooters also benefit from the ability to make first-round hits. Long-range rifle matches usually allow sighting shots to be taken at the start of the event. Typically, two sighters are allowed. If your first shot is fired just to see where it hits, that shot is wasted. If the shooter knows his distance and can alter his sights to take in the prevailing conditions and put his first round on target, he is definitely a step or two ahead of the other competitors, both in time and confidence. Proper time management and confidence win matches.

RANGE ESTIMATION FOR UNKNOWN DISTANCES

In attempting a first-round hit, the shooter must first know the range to the target. As the range to the target increases, it becomes more critical because of the increasing bullet drop. Estimating range by eye can be effective out to about 1/4-mile on 1-minute size targets. Varying terrain makes this more difficult because objects that are downhill appear farther away than objects that are uphill. Light conditions also play tricks on the human eye. Targets in excellent light appear much closer than targets that are in poor light conditions. Objects that are in sharp contrast to their surroundings appear closer than objects that blend in with their surroundings. At extreme ranges, range *estimates* aren't good enough. You must know the range precisely to produce a first-round hit. There are many rifle scope reticles that are designed to aid in range finding.

By knowing the size of the target you can use the bracketing system with a variable-power scope that has a duplex reticle. The magnification will determine how far you can range find. With the scope set on its lowest power setting, check the measurement of the duplex reticle. Check from post to post while viewing a target of known size at 200 yards. Place a 36-inch square target up to measure against.

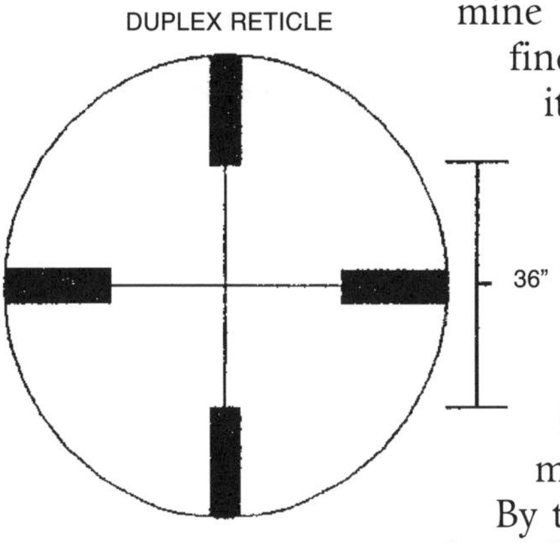

DUPLEX RETICLE

36"

By turning the scope's power ring, adjust the reticle until it just brackets the 36-inch target post to post. Mark the power ring with a dab of paint or by scribing for reference. Now move the target out to 300 yards and repeat this procedure. Continue moving the target out and range finding as far as the variable power feature will allow. With the extreme variable power scopes (4X to 16X or 6X to 24X) you can range find from 200 to 1,000 yards and even beyond. If your measurement is 36 inches with a full duplex post to post, half of this measurement (cross hair to post) is 18 inches. By knowing the target's size and bracketing the target, reading the marks on your scope's power ring will tell you the range. The Redfield Accurange scope uses a bracketing system that has the range scale built right into the scope. However, this scope only allows ranging out to 600 yards.

MIL DOT RETICLE

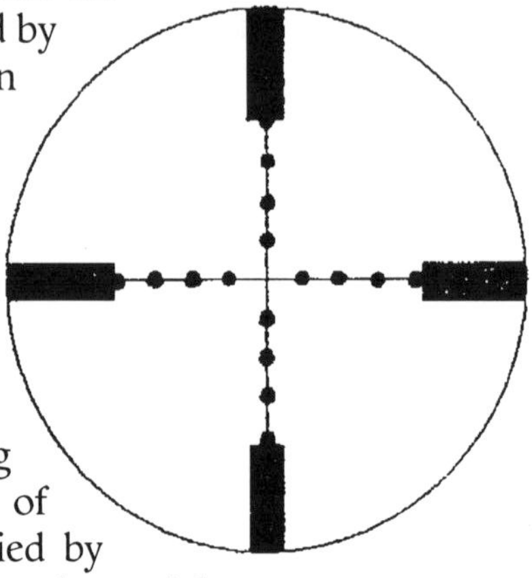

The mil dot duplex reticle for range finding was developed by the U.S. Marines for use on their sniper rifles. This system uses a series of .75-minute dots placed along the cross hairs. These dots are 1 millimeter apart and equal to 3.3 MOA in a fixed 10X scope. The formula for finding range is the known height of the target in yards multiplied by 1,000 and then divided by the reticle measured height of the target in mils. If you had an elk in the cross hairs and he measured 2.5 mils, you would multiply 1.5 (an elk is about 4 1/2 feet tall from its back to the ground, which is 1.5 yards) by 1,000, which equals 1,500. You then divide by 2.5 mils. The result is 600 yards (1.5 x 1,000 = 1,500; 1,500 ÷ 2.5 = 600). A hand calculator is standard issue for Marine snipers.

Next we go to the newly developed laser range finders. Bushnell makes the Lytespeed 400. It features a 4X constant focus monocular and runs on a 9-volt battery. It measures range from 15 to 400 yards and uses infrared energy pulses that are reflected back from the target. The range is read on a digital display in the view finder. It is accurate to +/- 1 yard at 400 yards.

The state of the art of personal range finding equipment is the Leica Geovid. This wonderful device combines 7 x 42 binoculars with laser range finding out to 1,100 yards +/- 1 yard. It is also available with a digital compass. However, these fine German optics do not come cheap. (The cost of the compass model is about $3,000.) It is the most accurate portable laser range finder/compass/binocular available. It weighs about 1.5 pounds and runs on a 6-volt lithium battery, which is supposed to be good for about 1,000 measurements. This instrument and the inevitable competition will take much of the guesswork out of range finding, thus translating to hits.

WIND ESTIMATION WITHOUT FLAGS

Once the range has been found, the shooter must then concentrate on wind and how it will affect the shot. First, wind direction must be determined. There are several different ways to determine direction when there are no flags to look at, such as holding up a wet finger, watching smoke, and feeling the air on your face and clothing. In addition, trees bend and move with the direction of air movement. When clouds are present they move with the general wind direction, although the higher the clouds the greater the chance of wind direction being different closer to the ground. Checking the wave direction of open water is yet another way to determine wind direction.

Next, the speed must be determined. A light breeze of 1 to 3 mph can hardly be felt, yet smoke will drift. Breezes from approximately 3 to 6 mph can be felt and your hair begins to move. With wind from 5 to 10 mph leaves and tree limbs begin moving. At 10 to 15 mph it causes trees to sway slightly, and dust and loose, light debris move and swirl. If the shooter keeps a hand-held wind-speed meter handy and keeps track of wind speed on occasion, he will always have a general idea of wind speed.

MIRAGE

Mirage refers to the waviness seen in the air over a direct or reflective heat source. It is caused by rising air of one temperature mixing with ambient air of another temperature. Air density is different at different temperatures and refracts light differently, resulting in the wavy patterns in the air. Virtually any time the sun is out, mirage will be visible. Mirage is not a good indicator of how much wind there is, but it is an excellent indicator of changes in wind speed.

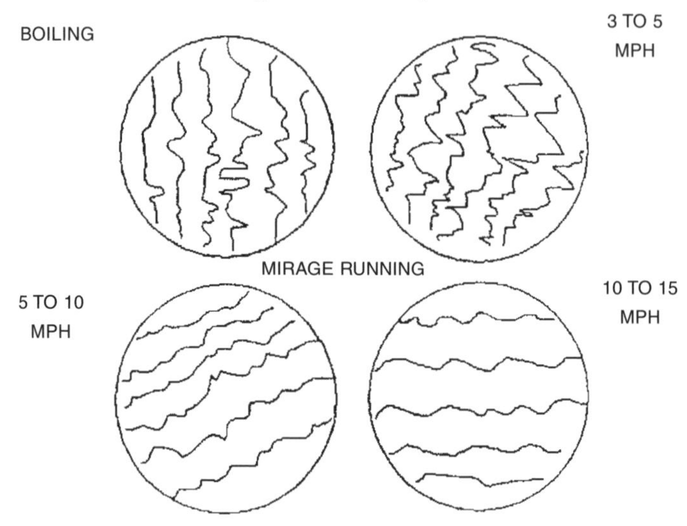

A good spotting scope is needed to see the details in the mirage necessary to use it as a change indicator. The columns of rising heated air are moved by the wind. With no wind, the mirage will look like wavy vertical lines going straight up. Sometimes when it is very hot, the mirage *boils*. The vertical lines become disturbed and give an appearance of boiling. There is actually enough pressure from the rising air and optical distortion from this phenomenon to cause the bullet to go high at long range, and under extreme conditions right over the target.

As the wind starts to blow, the vertical lines of the mirage start to lie over and run left or right depending on wind direction. The shooter must be aware of the actual wind direction and its relation to mirage. If the wind is straight from behind or straight from in front, the mirage will appear to boil or go straight up because it is being blown straight at or away from the shooter. To use mirage to sense changes in the wind in these conditions, turn the spotting scope slightly, and the mirage will appear to run because the shooter is no longer looking at the mirage waves straight on. If the wind is coming across your line of sight, the mirage will appear to run with the wind. The harder the wind blows, the more the mirage will lie over and run. After the wind reaches about 12 or 15 miles per hour, the mirage will run parallel to the ground and will no longer be a reliable indicator for detecting wind changes. The scope can be turned slightly into or with the wind to give the mirage more definition. Any visible change in mirage will require a sight correction to stay on target at long range. The only way to determine the value of the change is from experience while shooting in mirage.

Now that the shooter knows range, wind direction, and wind speed, he must calculate wind value. By using the clock system, he can determine the value as full-value, half-value, tail wind, or head wind; whether it's a half-value, he can determine if it is a tail wind or head wind half-value.

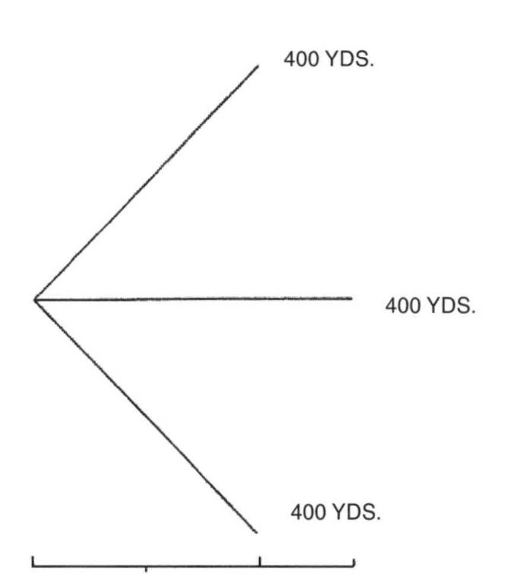

Time that gravity acts on bullets in level flight vs. bullets fired up or down.

SHOOTING ON A SLOPE

Extreme uphill or downhill shooting (more than 45

degrees) will require a small drop in elevation adjustment. This holds true for both uphill and downhill because as the elevation angle increases or decreases, the point of impact will always shift higher. This is due to the shorter linear distance in which gravity has to work on the bullet in flight.

EFFECTS OF WEATHER CONDITIONS

Weather conditions have a direct influence on bullet flight. Temperature, relative humidity, barometric pressure, and elevation changes all affect air density and will therefore influence trajectory and wind drift. To have any hope of producing a first-round hit, the shooter must have an understanding of these effects and how to compensate for the changes in point of impact. This is the reason the shooter must develop a standard load and settings to establish a performance baseline to make all sight corrections from.

Temperature Changes

An increase in temperature will cause the air to be less dense and will raise the point of impact. Conversely, a decrease in temperature will increase air density, which will lower bullet impact from a zero at standard conditions.

Another effect of temperature is on the performance of the ammunition. Hot ammunition (left in the sun or near a heater) can exhibit increased chamber pressures and velocities, which can cause bullet impact to be higher than under standard conditions. Likewise, cold ammunition may exhibit lower chamber pressures, and bullet impact may be lower than standard. Different smokeless powders are affected differently by temperature extremes. It is important to check the effects of temperature extremes on your specific loads by shooting in different conditions and recording the corrections.

Humidity Changes

Relative humidity has a small but significant effect on bullet flight. As relative humidity increases, actual air density decreases, which in turn raises the point of impact of the bullet higher than under standard conditions. Drier air is actually denser than air with moisture. Shooting in conditions drier than usual will make bullet impact lower.

These statements are contradicted by many publications. However, what these publications say about the relationship between humidity and air density just isn't so. If you ask your high school chemistry or physics teacher about laws governing gases, they will set you straight.

A classic example of this is when shooting late in the day. Recently one of us was out shooting, had the rifle zeroed at 800 yards, and had fired several groups. The sun was setting and the air temperature was beginning to drop. As the air cooled, relative humidity rapidly increased to near the dew point. As he began to shoot again, he noticed that the air was getting quite moist. When he fired, it was a miss on a 2-minute target. He had to come down 1 minute, and in the next 15 minutes, as the relative humidity increased, he had to come down another minute to remain on target. The reason the point of impact was rising was that as the relative humidity was rising, the air was becoming less dense. Less dense air slows the bullet down less and allows it to fly farther during its flight time. The humidity rise was more dramatic than the temperature drop effect because the dew point was close to the current temperature. If the dew point had been much lower, the drop in temperature would have caused a slightly lower point of impact. In this particular instance, the change in relative humidity moved the point of impact 16 inches at 800 yards and this change took place in only 30 minutes. Being aware of condition changes helps produce first-round hits.

Barometric Pressure Changes

Barometric pressure is the measurement of the weight of the atmosphere. The higher the barometric pressure reading, the denser the air. Denser air increases drag on a bullet in flight, making it slow down sooner and shortening the distance it will fly during its flight time. This will cause the point of impact to be lower than under standard conditions. Obviously the reverse is also true; the lower the barometric pressure reading, the higher the point of impact under standard conditions.

Elevation Changes

Elevation affects bullet flight too. This is related directly to barometric pressure. Higher elevations have air that is less dense than do lower elevations and this affects bullet flight in the same way. The lower drag on the bullet at higher elevations because of the thinner, less dense air raises the point of impact above the normal. At lower elevations, the air is denser, which increases bullet drag and lowers the point of impact below the normal.

THE REALITY OF PROFICIENT LONG-RANGE SHOOTING

So far we have discussed the hows and whys of practical long-range shooting. We have discussed range estimation, reading the wind and mirage, and the finer points of elevation and humidity. We have also discussed equipment and how to set it up. Having accurate information and equipment that you have confidence in are good first steps to becoming a proficient long-range shooter. However, don't succumb to the idea that books and gadgets can replace practice and experience. There is absolutely no substitute for practice and experience. One of the best places to get practice and experience is in NRA high-power rifle competition. Some such matches (the smaller ones) are run at reduced ranges of 100 or 200 yards, but regular across-the-course matches are run at 200, 300, and 600 yards. The course of fire is as follows:

- 20 shots standing at 200 yards in 20 minutes
- Two 10-shot strings of rapid-fire sitting at 200 yards in 60 seconds
- Two 10-shot strings of rapid-fire prone at 300 yards in 60 seconds
- 20 shots of slow fire prone at 600 yards in 20 minutes

You will meet some great people and be able to measure your ability to hit under pressure in changing conditions on demand. We cannot think of a better all-around test of a shooter's true ability than these matches. There are long-range high-power matches too, which are all slow-fire prone shot at either 600 or 1,000 yards. There is also the Palma Course, which consists of slow-fire prone at 800, 900, and 1,000 yards.

You may not be the champion, but win or lose, you will learn a great deal about hitting at long range. Even shooting from the bench at 100 yards is very good practice. The ability to get a good sight picture and have proper breathing control, good trigger squeeze, and follow-through are critical at any range. These skills are easily developed through 100-yard bench-rest shooting.

Remember, buying a book or two and lots of gadgets does not make you a competent shooter. Only practice combined with solid equipment and information can do that.

PRE-SHOT CHECKLIST

To make a first-round hit, the shooter must make the calculations. Here's a checklist that should be followed:

1. Know that your 100-yard zero is correct.
2. Calculate range to target.
3. Estimate wind speed.
4. Determine wind direction and value.
5. Determine temperature, elevation, relative humidity, and barometric pressure and their effect on air density.
6. Determine elevation angle.
7. Adjust scope.
8. Wait for shooting window.
9. Fire.
10. Hit.

Appendix A

Scope Adjustment Charts for Common Cartridges

These charts give the average rifleman a starting point for determining elevation and windage data for specific cartridges out to their maximum range, which is determined by the cartridge's supersonic capability. These data are based on sea-level standard atmospheric conditions (sea level with atmospheric pressure at 29.53 inches of mercury, temperature at 59 degrees Fahrenheit, and relative humidity at 78 percent).

This information provides a good starting point for developing real data for your specific rifle and load. As you start shooting and adjust the data for your elevation and conditions, maintain a log with your scope adjustment range charts.

All charts listed here are based on a scope 1.5 inches above the bore, except for the AR-15 .223 Remington (3.75 inches), SKS 7.62 x 39 carbine (2.2 inches), M1A/M14 7.62 (2 inches), Dragunov 7.62 x 54 (2.2 inches), Enfield .303 British (2 inches), and Rib Mountain Arms .50-caliber BMG (2.4 inches).

SCOPE ADJUSTMENT CHART IN MOA		
NOTES:		
CARTRIDGE: .223 REMINGTON (5.56MM NATO)		
BULLET: 52-GRAIN BOATTAIL HOLLOWPOINT		
VELOCITY: 3,300 FPS		
RANGE	**+ ELEV -**	**10 mph**
IN YARDS	**IN MINUTES**	**L WIND R**
100	0.0	1.25
200	+1.5	2.5
300	+3.75	4.25
350	+5.25	5.0
400	+7.0	6.0
450	+9.0	7.25
500	+11.5	8.5
550	+14.0	9.75
600	+17.25	11.25

SCOPE ADJUSTMENT CHART IN MOA		
NOTES: AR-15		
CARTRIDGE: .223 REMINGTON (5.56MM NATO)		
BULLET: 55-GRAIN FMJ BOATTAIL		
VELOCITY: 3,000 FPS		
RANGE	**+ ELEV -**	**10 mph**
IN YARDS	**IN MINUTES**	**L WIND R**
100	0.0	1.0
200	+2.5	2.5
300	+3.0	4.25
350	+4.75	5.25
400	+6.75	6.25
450	+9.0	7.5
500	+11.5	8.5
550	+14.5	9.75
600	+17.75	11.0

SCOPE ADJUSTMENT CHART IN MOA		
NOTES:		
CARTRIDGE: .223 REMINGTON (5.56MM NATO)		
BULLET: 55-GRAIN BOATTAIL SPITZER		
VELOCITY: 3,200 FPS		
RANGE	**+ ELEV -**	**10 mph**
IN YARDS	**IN MINUTES**	**L WIND R**
100	0.0	1.0
200	+1.5	2.5
300	+4.0	3.75
350	+5.5	4.5
400	+7.0	5.5
450	+9.0	6.5
500	+11.25	7.5
550	+13.75	8.75
600	+16.5	10.0
650	+19.75	11.25
700	+23.25	12.5

SCOPE ADJUSTMENT CHART IN MOA		
NOTES: AR-15 1-IN-9 TWIST		
CARTRIDGE: .223 REMINGTON (5.56MM NATO)		
BULLET: 69-GRAIN BOATTAIL HOLLOWPOINT		
VELOCITY: 2,850 FPS		
RANGE	**+ ELEV -**	**10 mph**
IN YARDS	**IN MINUTES**	**L WIND R**
100	0.0	2.25
200	+.75	3.25
300	+3.25	3.5
350	+9.75	4.25
400	+6.75	5.0
450	+8.5	5.75
500	+11.0	6.5
550	+13.25	7.5
600	+16.0	8.25
650	+19.0	9.25
700	+22.25	10.25
750	+26.0	11.25
800	+30.0	12.5

SCOPE ADJUSTMENT CHART IN MOA		
NOTES: AR-15 1-IN-7 TWIST		
CARTRIDGE: .223 REMINGTON (5.56MM NATO)		
BULLET: 80-GRAIN BOATTAIL HOLLOWPOINT		
VELOCITY: 2,750 FPS		
RANGE	**+ ELEV -**	**10 mph**
IN YARDS	**IN MINUTES**	**L WIND R**
100	0.0	.075
200	+0.75	1.75
300	+3.25	2.5
350	+4.75	3.0
400	+6.25	3.5
450	+8.0	4.0
500	+10.0	4.75
550	+12.0	5.5
600	+14.5	6.0
650	+16.75	6.75
700	+19.5	7.5
750	+22.25	8.25
800	+25.5	9.00
850	+28.75	9.75
900	+32.25	10.5
950	+36.25	11.5
1,000	+40.5	12.25

SCOPE ADJUSTMENT CHART IN MOA		
NOTES:		
CARTRIDGE: .22-250 REMINGTON		
BULLET: 52-GRAIN BOATTAIL HOLLOWPOINT		
VELOCITY: 3,750 FPS		
RANGE	**+ ELEV -**	**10 mph**
IN YARDS	**IN MINUTES**	**L WIND R**
100	0.0	1.0
200	+1.0	2.25
300	+2.5	3.5
350	+3.75	4.25
400	+5.0	5.0
450	+6.5	6.0
500	+8.25	7.0
550	+10.0	8.0
600	+12.25	9.25
650	+15.0	10.5
700	+17.75	11.75
750	+21.25	13.25

SCOPE ADJUSTMENT CHART IN MOA		
NOTES:		
CARTRIDGE: .22-250 REMINGTON		
BULLET: 55-GRAIN BOATTAIL SPITZER		
VELOCITY: 3,670 FPS		
RANGE	**+ ELEV -**	**10 mph**
IN YARDS	**IN MINUTES**	**L WIND R**
100	0.0	1.0
200	+1.0	2.0
300	+2.5	3.25
350	+3.75	3.75
400	+5.0	4.5
450	+6.25	5.25
500	+7.75	6.0
550	+9.5	7.0
600	+11.5	8.0
650	+13.75	9.0
700	+16.5	10.25
750	+19.25	11.25
800	+22.5	12.5

SCOPE ADJUSTMENT CHART IN MOA		
NOTES:		
CARTRIDGE: .243 WINCHESTER		
BULLET: 70-GRAIN BOATTAIL HOLLOWPOINT		
VELOCITY: 3,400 FPS		
RANGE	**+ ELEV -**	**10 mph**
IN YARDS	**IN MINUTES**	**L WIND R**
100	0.0	1.0
200	+1.25	2.0
300	+3.25	3.25
350	+4.5	4.0
400	+6.0	4.75
450	+7.5	5.5
500	+8.5	6.25
550	+11.25	7.25
600	+13.5	8.25
650	+15.75	9.25
700	+18.5	10.25
750	+21.75	11.25
800	+25.25	12.5

SCOPE ADJUSTMENT CHART IN MOA		
NOTES:		
CARTRIDGE: .243 WINCHESTER		
BULLET: 85-GRAIN HOLLOWPOINT		
VELOCITY: 3,200 FPS		
RANGE	**+ ELEV -**	**10 mph**
IN YARDS	**IN MINUTES**	**L WIND R**
L WIND R		
100	0.0	1.0
200	+1.5	2.0
300	+3.5	3.25
350	+5.0	4.0
400	+6.5	4.5
450	+8.25	5.25
500	+10.0	6.0
550	+12.0	6.75
600	+14.25	7.5
650	+16.75	8.5
700	+19.5	9.5
750	+22.5	10.5
800	+25.75	11.5

SCOPE ADJUSTMENT CHART IN MOA		
NOTES:		
CARTRIDGE: .243 WINCHESTER		
BULLET: 100-GRAIN SPITZER BOATTAIL		
VELOCITY: 2,950 FPS		
RANGE	+ ELEV -	10 mph
IN YARDS	IN MINUTES	L WIND R
100	0.0	.75
200	+1.5	1.5
300	+4.0	2.25
350	+5.25	2.75
400	+6.75	3.25
450	+8.25	3.75
500	+10.0	4.25
550	+11.75	4.75
600	+13.75	5.5
650	+15.75	6.0
700	+18.0	6.5
750	+20.25	7.25
800	+23.0	8.0
850	+25.75	8.75
900	+28.75	9.5
950	+32.0	10.25
1,000	+35.5	11.0

SCOPE ADJUSTMENT CHART IN MOA		
NOTES:		
CARTRIDGE: 6MM REMINGTON		
BULLET: 80-GRAIN SPITZER BOATTAIL		
VELOCITY: 3,470 FPS		
RANGE	**+ ELEV -**	**10 mph**
IN YARDS	**IN MINUTES**	**L WIND R**
100	0.0	.75
200	+1.0	1.5
300	+2.75	2.5
350	+3.75	3.0
400	+5.0	3.5
450	+6.25	4.25
500	+7.75	4.75
550	+9.25	5.5
600	+11.0	6.25
650	+12.75	7.0
700	+14.75	7.75
750	+17.25	8.5
800	+19.75	9.5
850	+22.5	10.25
900	+25.5	11.5
950	+29.0	12.5
1,000	+32.75	13.5

SCOPE ADJUSTMENT CHART IN MOA		
NOTES:		
CARTRIDGE: 6MM REMINGTON		
BULLET: 100-GRAIN SPITZER BOATTAIL		
VELOCITY: 3,100 FPS		
RANGE	**+ ELEV -**	**10 mph**
IN YARDS	**IN MINUTES**	**L WIND R**
100	0.0	.75
200	+1.25	1.25
300	+3.5	2.25
350	+4.5	2.5
400	+6.0	3.0
450	+7.25	3.5
500	+8.75	4.0
550	+10.5	4.5
600	+12.25	5.0
650	+14.0	5.5
700	+16.0	6.0
750	+18.0	6.25
800	+19.25	7.0
850	+23.0	8.0
900	+25.5	8.75
950	+28.5	9.5

SCOPE ADJUSTMENT CHART IN MOA		
NOTES: CON'T FROM PAGE 99		
CARTRIDGE: 6MM REMINGTON		
BULLET: 100-GRAIN SPITZER BOATTAIL		
VELOCITY: 3100 FPS		
RANGE	**+ ELEV -**	**10 mph**
IN YARDS	**IN MINUTES**	**L WIND R**
1,000	+31.5	10.25
1,050	+35.0	11.0
1,100	+38.5	12.0

SCOPE ADJUSTMENT CHART IN MOA		
NOTES: 1-IN-8 TWIST		
CARTRIDGE: 6MM REMINGTON		
BULLET: 107-GRAIN BOATTAIL HOLLOWPOINT		
VELOCITY: 3,000 FPS		
RANGE	**+ ELEV -**	**10 mph**
IN YARDS	**IN MINUTES**	**L WIND R**
100	0.0	.5
200	+1.25	1.00
300	+3.25	1.75
350	+4.5	2.0
400	+5.75	2.5
450	+7.0	2.75
500	+8.5	3.0
550	+9.75	3.5
600	+11.25	3.75
650	+13.0	4.25
700	+14.75	4.5
750	+16.5	5
800	+18.25	5.5
850	+20.25	6.0
900	+22.5	6.5
950	+24.5	6.75

SCOPE ADJUSTMENT CHART IN MOA		
NOTES: CON'T FROM PAGE 101		
CARTRIDGE: 6MM REMINGTON		
BULLET: 107-GRAIN BOATTAIL HOLLOWPOINT		
VELOCITY: 3,000 FPS		
RANGE	**+ ELEV -**	**10 mph**
IN YARDS	**IN MINUTES**	**L WIND R**
1,000	+27.0	7.5
1,050	+29.5	8
1,100	+32.0	8.5
1,150	+35.0	9.0
1,200	+37.75	9.5
1,250	+41.0	10.25
1,300	+44.25	10.75
1,350	+47.75	11.5
1,400	+51.5	12.0

SCOPE ADJUSTMENT CHART IN MOA		
NOTES:		
CARTRIDGE: .25-06 REMINGTON		
BULLET: 75-GRAIN HOLLOWPOINT		
VELOCITY: 3,700 FPS		
RANGE	**+ ELEV -**	**10 mph**
IN YARDS	**IN MINUTES**	**L WIND R**
100	0.0	1.25
200	+1.0	2.75
300	+3.0	4.25
350	+4.25	5.25
400	+6.0	6.25
450	+7.75	7.5
500	+9.75	8.75
550	+12.25	10.0
600	+15.0	11.5
650	+18.25	12.75
700	+22.0	14.25

SCOPE ADJUSTMENT CHART IN MOA		
NOTES:		
CARTRIDGE: .25-06 REMINGTON		
BULLET: 100-GRAIN BOATTAIL SPITZER		
VELOCITY: 3,230 FPS		
RANGE	**+ ELEV -**	**10 mph**
IN YARDS	**IN MINUTES**	**L WIND R**
100	0.0	.75
200	+1.25	1.5
300	+3.25	2.5
350	+4.5	3.0
400	+5.75	3.5
450	+7.25	4.0
500	+8.75	4.75
550	+10.5	5.5
600	+12.25	6.0
650	+14.25	6.75
700	+16.5	7.5
750	+19.0	8.5
800	+21.5	9.25
850	+24.5	10.25
900	+27.75	11.0
950	+31.5	12.0
1,000	+35.25	13.0

SCOPE ADJUSTMENT CHART IN MOA		
NOTES:		
CARTRIDGE: .25-06 REMINGTON		
BULLET: 117-GRAIN BOATTAIL SPITZER		
VELOCITY: 2,990 FPS		
RANGE	**+ ELEV -**	**10 mph**
IN YARDS	**IN MINUTES**	**L WIND R**
100	+0.0	.75
200	+1.5	1.5
300	+3.75	2.25
350	+5.25	2.75
400	+6.5	3.25
450	+8.0	3.75
500	+9.75	4.25
550	+11.5	4.75
600	+13.25	5.5
650	+15.5	6.0
700	+17.75	6.75
750	+20.0	7.25
800	+22.5	8.0
850	+25.5	8.75
900	+28.5	9.5
950	+31.75	10.5
1,000	+38.5	11.25

SCOPE ADJUSTMENT CHART IN MOA		
NOTES:		
CARTRIDGE: .257 WEATHERBY MAGNUM		
BULLET: 75-GRAIN HOLLOWPOINT		
VELOCITY: 3,900 FPS		
RANGE	**+ ELEV -**	**10 mph**
IN YARDS	**IN MINUTES**	**L WIND R**
100	0.0	1.25
200	+1.0	2.5
300	+2.5	4.0
350	+3.75	5.0
400	+5.25	6.0
450	+6.75	7.0
500	+8.5	8.0
550	+10.75	9.25
600	+13.25	10.5
650	+16.0	12.0
700	+19.5	13.5

SCOPE ADJUSTMENT CHART IN MOA		
NOTES:		
CARTRIDGE: .257 WEATHERBY MAGNUM		
BULLET: 120-GRAIN SPITZER BOATTAIL		
VELOCITY: 3,200 FPS		
RANGE	**+ ELEV -**	**10 mph**
IN YARDS	**IN MINUTES**	**L WIND R**
100	0.0	.5
200	+1.5	1.25
300	+3.0	2.0
350	+4.25	2.25
400	+5.5	2.5
450	+6.75	3.0
500	+8.0	3.5
550	+9.5	4.0
600	+11.0	4.5
650	+12.5	5.0
700	+14.25	5.25
750	+16.0	5.75
800	+18.0	6.25
850	+20.25	7.0
900	+22.5	7.5
950	+24.75	8.0

SCOPE ADJUSTMENT CHART IN MOA		
NOTES: CON'T FROM PAGE 107		
CARTRIDGE: .257 WEATHERBY MAGNUM		
BULLET: 120-GRAIN SPITZER BOATTAIL		
VELOCITY: 3,200 FPS		
RANGE	**+ ELEV -**	**10 mph**
IN YARDS	**IN MINUTES**	**L WIND R**
1,000	+27.25	8.5
1,050	+30.0	9.25
1,100	+33.0	10.0
1,150	+36.0	10.5
1,200	+39.5	11.25
1,250	+43.0	12.0
1,300	+46.75	12.75

SCOPE ADJUSTMENT CHART IN MOA		
NOTES: 1-IN-8 TWIST		
CARTRIDGE: 6.5MM X 55		
BULLET: 140-GRAIN SPITZER BOATTAIL		
VELOCITY: 2,500 FPS		
RANGE	**+ ELEV -**	**10 mph**
IN YARDS	**IN MINUTES**	**L WIND R**
100	0.0	.75
200	+2.5	1.5
300	+5.75	2.5
350	+7.5	3.0
400	+9.5	3.5
450	+11.75	4.0
500	+14.0	4.5
550	+16.25	5.0
600	+18.75	5.5
650	+21.5	6.25
700	+24.5	6.75
750	+27.25	7.5
800	+30.5	8.25
850	+34.0	9.0
900	+37.75	9.5
950	+41.75	10.25
1,000	+50.0	11.0

SCOPE ADJUSTMENT CHART IN MOA		
NOTES: 1-IN-8 TWIST		
CARTRIDGE: 6.5MM-06		
BULLET: 155-GRAIN HOLLOWPOINT BOATTAIL		
VELOCITY: 2,800 FPS		
RANGE	**+ ELEV -**	**10 mph**
IN YARDS	**IN MINUTES**	**L WIND R**
100	0.0	.5
200	+1.75	1.25
300	+4.25	1.75
350	+5.5	2.25
400	+7.0	2.5
450	+8.5	3.0
500	+10.25	3.25
550	+12.0	3.5
600	+13.5	4.0
650	+15.5	4.5
700	+17.5	5.0
750	+19.5	5.25
800	+21.75	5.75
850	+24.0	6.25
900	+26.5	6.75
950	+29.0	7.25
1,000	+31.75	7.75

1,050	+34.75	8.25
1,100	+37.75	8.75
1,150	+41.0	9.25
1,200	+44.25	10.0
1,250	+47.75	10.5
1,300	+51.5	11.0

SCOPE ADJUSTMENT CHART IN MOA		
NOTES:		
CARTRIDGE: .264 WINCHESTER MAGNUM		
BULLET: 85-GRAIN HOLLOWPOINT		
VELOCITY: 3,400 FPS		
RANGE	**+ ELEV -**	**10 mph**
IN YARDS	**IN MINUTES**	**L WIND R**
100	0.0	1.25
200	+1.5	2.5
300	+3.5	3.75
350	+4.75	4.75
400	+6.25	5.5
450	+8.0	6.5
500	+10.0	7.5
550	+12.25	8.5
600	+14.75	9.5
650	+17.5	10.5
700	+20.75	11.75

SCOPE ADJUSTMENT CHART IN MOA		
NOTES:		
CARTRIDGE: .264 WINCHESTER MAGNUM		
BULLET: 120-GRAIN SPITZER		
VELOCITY: 3,200 FPS		
RANGE	**+ ELEV -**	**10 mph**
IN YARDS	**IN MINUTES**	**L WIND R**
100	0.0	.75
200	+1.25	1.5
300	+3.25	2.25
350	+4.5	2.75
400	+5.75	3.25
450	+7.0	3.75
500	+8.75	4.25
550	+10.25	5.0
600	+12.0	5.5
650	+13.75	6.25
700	+15.75	6.75
750	+18.0	7.25
800	+20.25	8.0
850	+22.75	8.5
900	+25.5	9.25
950	+28.5	10.0

SCOPE ADJUSTMENT CHART IN MOA		
NOTES: CON'T FROM PAGE 113		
CARTRIDGE: .264 WINCHESTER MAGNUM		
BULLET: 120-GRAIN SPITZER		
VELOCITY: 3,200 FPS		
RANGE	**+ ELEV -**	**10 mph**
IN YARDS	**IN MINUTES**	**L WIND R**
1,000	+31.5	10.75
1,050	+35.0	11.5
1,100	+38.75	12.5

SCOPE ADJUSTMENT CHART IN MOA		
NOTES:		
CARTRIDGE: .264 WINCHESTER MAGNUM		
BULLET: 140-GRAIN SPITZER		
VELOCITY: 3,030 FPS		
RANGE	**+ ELEV -**	**10 mph**
IN YARDS	**IN MINUTES**	**L WIND R**
100	0.0	.5
200	+1.5	1.0
300	+3.5	1.75
350	+4.5	2.0
400	+6.0	2.25
450	+7.25	2.75
500	+8.5	3.0
550	+10.0	3.5
600	+11.5	3.75
650	+13.25	4.25
700	+15.0	4.5
750	+16.75	5.0
800	+18.75	5.5
850	+20.75	6.0
900	+22.75	6.5
950	+25.0	7.0

SCOPE ADJUSTMENT CHART IN MOA		
NOTES: CON'T FROM PAGE 115		
CARTRIDGE: .264 WINCHESTER MAGNUM		
BULLET: 140-GRAIN SPITZER		
VELOCITY: 3,030 FPS		
RANGE	**+ ELEV -**	**10 mph**
IN YARDS	**IN MINUTES**	**L WIND R**
1,000	+27.5	7.5
1,050	+30.0	8.0
1,100	+32.5	8.5
1,150	+35.5	9.0
1,200	+38.5	9.5
1,250	+41.75	10.25
1,300	+45.0	10.75
1,350	+48.5	11.5
1,400	+52.25	12.0

SCOPE ADJUSTMENT CHART IN MOA		
NOTES:		
CARTRIDGE: .270 WINCHESTER		
BULLET: 90-GRAIN SPITZER		
VELOCITY: 3,400 FPS		
RANGE	**+ ELEV -**	**10 mph**
IN YARDS	**IN MINUTES**	**L WIND R**
100	0.0	1.25
200	+1.25	2.75
300	+3.75	4.5
350	+5.25	5.5
400	+7.0	6.5
450	+9.0	7.75
500	+11.25	8.75
550	+14.0	10.0
600	+17.0	11.25
650	+20.25	12.75
700	+24.25	14.0

SCOPE ADJUSTMENT CHART IN MOA		
NOTES:		
CARTRIDGE: .270 WINCHESTER		
BULLET: 135-GRAIN BOATTAIL HOLLOWPOINT		
VELOCITY: 3,000 FPS		
RANGE	**+ ELEV -**	**10 mph**
IN YARDS	**IN MINUTES**	**L WIND R**
100	0.0	.5
200	+1.5	1.25
300	+3.5	2.0
350	+4.75	2.25
400	+6.25	2.75
450	+7.75	3.25
500	+9.25	3.5
550	+10.75	4.0
600	+12.5	4.5
650	+14.25	5.0
700	+16.25	5.5
750	+18.25	6.0
800	+20.5	6.5
850	+22.75	7.0
900	+25.25	7.75
950	+28.0	8.5
1,000	+30.75	9.0

1,050	+33.75	9.75
1,100	+37.0	10.5
1,150	+40.5	11.25
1,200	+44.5	12.0

SCOPE ADJUSTMENT CHART IN MOA		
NOTES:		
CARTRIDGE: .270 WINCHESTER		
BULLET: 150-GRAIN BOATTAIL SPITZER		
VELOCITY: 2,850 FPS		
RANGE	**+ ELEV -**	**10 mph**
IN YARDS	**IN MINUTES**	**L WIND R**
100	0.0	.75
200	+1.75	1.5
300	+4.25	2.0
350	+5.5	2.5
400	+7.0	3.0
450	+8.5	3.5
500	+10.25	4.0
550	+12.25	4.5
600	+14.0	5.0
650	+16.0	5.5
700	+18.25	6.0
750	+20.5	6.5
800	+23.0	7.0
850	+25.75	7.75
900	+28.5	8.25
950	+31.5	9.0

1,000	+34.75	9.75
1,050	+38.25	10.5
1,100	+42.0	11.25

SCOPE ADJUSTMENT CHART IN MOA		
NOTES:		
CARTRIDGE: 7MM X 57 MAUSER		
BULLET: 140-GRAIN BOATTAIL SPITZER		
VELOCITY: 2,660 FPS		
RANGE	**+ ELEV -**	**10 mph**
IN YARDS	**IN MINUTES**	**L WIND R**
100	0.0	.75
200	+2.25	1.75
300	+5.25	2.75
350	+6.75	3.25
400	+8.75	3.75
450	+10.75	4.5
500	+12.75	5.0
550	+15.0	5.5
600	+17.5	6.25
650	+20.25	7.0
700	+23.0	7.75
750	+26.0	8.5
800	+29.25	9.25
850	+32.75	10.0
900	+36.5	10.5
950	+40.5	11.5
1,000	+44.75	12.25

SCOPE ADJUSTMENT CHART IN MOA		
NOTES:		
CARTRIDGE: 7MM-08 REMINGTON		
BULLET: 150-GRAIN BOATTAIL HOLLOWPOINT		
VELOCITY: 2,715 FPS		
RANGE	**+ ELEV -**	**10 mph**
IN YARDS	**IN MINUTES**	**L WIND R**
100	0.0	.75
200	+2.0	1.75
300	+4.75	2.5
350	+6.5	3.0
400	+8.25	3.5
450	+10.0	4.0
500	+12.0	4.5
550	+14.25	5.25
600	+16.5	5.75
650	+18.75	6.5
700	+21.5	7.0
750	+24.25	7.75
800	+27.25	8.5
850	+30.5	9.0
900	+33.75	9.75
950	+37.5	10.5
1,000	+41.25	11.25

SCOPE ADJUSTMENT CHART IN MOA		
NOTES:		
CARTRIDGE: .280 REMINGTON		
BULLET: 150-GRAIN BOATTAIL HOLLOWPOINT		
VELOCITY: 2,890 FPS		
RANGE	+ ELEV -	10 mph
IN YARDS	IN MINUTES	L WIND R
100	0.0	.75
200	+1.75	1.5
300	+4.25	2.25
350	+5.5	2.75
400	+7.0	3.25
450	+8.5	3.75
500	+10.5	4.25
550	+12.25	4.75
600	+14.25	5.25
650	+16.25	5.75
700	+18.5	6.5
750	+21.0	7.0
800	+23.5	7.75
850	+26.25	8.25
900	+29.25	9.0
950	+32.25	9.75

1,000	+35.75	10.5
1,050	+39.25	11.25
1,100	+43.25	12.0

SCOPE ADJUSTMENT CHART IN MOA		
NOTES:		
CARTRIDGE: 7MM REMINGTON MAGNUM		
BULLET: 150-GRAIN BOATTAIL HOLLOWPOINT		
VELOCITY: 3,110 FPS		
RANGE	**+ ELEV -**	**10 mph**
IN YARDS	**IN MINUTES**	**L WIND R**
100	0.0	.75
200	+1.25	1.25
300	+3.5	2.0
350	+4.5	2.5
400	+5.75	3.0
450	+7.25	3.25
500	+8.75	3.75
550	+10.25	4.25
600	+12.0	4.75
650	+13.75	5.25
700	+15.5	5.75
750	+17.5	6.25
800	+19.75	7.0
850	+22.0	7.5
900	+24.5	8.0
950	+27.25	8.75
1,000	+30.0	9.5

1,050	+33.0	10.0
1,100	+36.25	10.75
1,150	+39.75	11.5
1,200	+43.5	12.25

SCOPE ADJUSTMENT CHART IN MOA		
NOTES:		
CARTRIDGE: 7MM REMINGTON MAGNUM		
BULLET: 168-GRAIN BOATTAIL HOLLOWPOINT		
VELOCITY: 2,900 FPS		
RANGE	**+ ELEV -**	**10 mph**
IN YARDS	**IN MINUTES**	**L WIND R**
100	0.0	.5
200	+1.5	1.25
300	+4.0	2.0
350	+5.25	2.25
400	+6.75	2.75
450	+8.25	3.25
500	+9.75	3.5
550	+11.5	4.0
600	+13.25	4.5
650	+15.25	5.0
700	+17.25	5.5
750	+19.25	6.0
800	+21.5	6.5
850	+24.0	7.0
900	+26.5	7.5
950	+29.25	8.25
1,000	+32.0	8.75

1,050	+35.0	9.25
1,100	+38.25	10.0
1,150	+41.75	10.75
1,200	+45.5	11.25

SCOPE ADJUSTMENT CHART IN MOA		
NOTES:		
CARTRIDGE: 7MM STW		
BULLET: 168-GRAIN BOATTAIL HOLLOWPOINT		
VELOCITY: 3,300 FPS		
RANGE	+ ELEV -	10 mph
IN YARDS	IN MINUTES	L WIND R
100	+0.0	.5
200	+1.0	1.0
300	+2.75	1.75
350	+3.75	2.0
400	+5.0	2.25
450	+6.0	2.5
500	+7.25	3.0
550	+8.25	3.25
600	+9.75	3.5
650	+11.25	4.0
700	+12.75	4.5
750	+14.25	5.0
800	+15.75	5.25
850	+17.75	5.75
900	+19.5	6.25
950	+21.5	6.75
1,000	+23.5	7.25

1,050	+25.75	7.75
1,100	+28.25	8.25
1,150	+30.75	8.75
1,200	+33.25	9.5
1,250	+36.25	10.0
1,300	+39.25	10.5
1,350	+42.5	11.25
1,400	+46.0	11.75
1,450	+49.5	12.5
1,500	+53.25	13.25

SCOPE ADJUSTMENT CHART IN MOA		
NOTES: SKS CARBINE WITH SCOPE		
CARTRIDGE: 7.62MM X 39 RUSSIAN		
BULLET: 123-GRAIN FMJ		
VELOCITY: 2,365 FPS		
RANGE	**+ ELEV -**	**10 mph**
IN YARDS	**IN MINUTES**	**L WIND R**
100	0.0	1.75
200	+3.0	3.5
300	+7.75	5.5
350	+10.75	7.0
400	+14.0	8.25
450	+17.75	9.5
500	+22.0	10.75

SCOPE ADJUSTMENT CHART IN MOA		
NOTES: DRAGUNOV RIFLE/MOSIN-NAGANT		
CARTRIDGE: 7.62MM X 54 RUSSIAN		
BULLET: 150-GRAIN FMJ		
VELOCITY: 2,800 FPS		
RANGE	**+ ELEV -**	**10 mph**
IN YARDS	**IN MINUTES**	**L WIND R**
100	0.0	.75
200	+1.5	1.75
300	+4.25	2.5
350	+5.5	3.25
400	+7.25	3.75
450	+9.0	4.25
500	+11.0	5.0
550	+13.0	5.5
600	+15.5	6.25
650	+17.75	6.75
700	+20.5	7.5
750	+23.25	8.25
800	+26.5	9.5
850	+29.5	10.0
900	+33.25	10.75
950	+37.25	11.5
1,000	+41.25	12.5

SCOPE ADJUSTMENT CHART IN MOA		
NOTES:		
CARTRIDGE: 7.62MM NATO (.308 WINCHESTER)		
BULLET: 147-GRAIN FMJ BOATTAIL		
VELOCITY: 2,820 FPS		
RANGE	**+ ELEV -**	**10 mph**
IN YARDS	**IN MINUTES**	**L WIND R**
100	0.0	.75
200	+1.75	1.5
300	+4.25	2.5
350	+6.0	3.0
400	+7.5	3.5
450	+9.25	4.0
500	+11.25	4.5
550	+13.25	5.0
600	+15.25	5.75
650	+17.5	6.25
700	+20.0	7.0
750	+22.5	7.5
800	+25.5	8.5
850	+28.5	9.0
900	+31.75	9.75
950	+35.25	10.5
1,000	+39.25	11.5

SCOPE ADJUSTMENT CHART IN MOA		
NOTES:		
CARTRIDGE: 7.62MM NATO (.308 WINCHESTER)		
BULLET: 155-GRAIN BOATTAIL HOLLOWPOINT		
VELOCITY: 2,800 FPS		
RANGE	**+ ELEV -**	**10 mph**
IN YARDS	**IN MINUTES**	**L WIND R**
100	0.0	.75
200	+1.75	1.5
300	+4.5	2.25
350	+6.0	2.75
400	+7.5	3.25
450	+9.25	3.75
500	+11.0	4.25
550	+13.0	4.75
600	+15.0	5.25
650	+17.25	6.0
700	+19.5	6.5
750	+22.25	7.25
800	+25.0	7.75
850	+27.75	8.5
900	+31.0	9.25
950	+34.5	10.0

SCOPE ADJUSTMENT CHART IN MOA		
NOTES: CON'T FROM PAGE 135		
CARTRIDGE: 7.62MM NATO (.308 WINCHESTER)		
BULLET: 155-GRAIN BOATTAIL HOLLOWPOINT		
VELOCITY: 2,800 FPS		
RANGE	**+ ELEV -**	**10 mph**
IN YARDS	**IN MINUTES**	**L WIND R**
1,000	+38.0	10.75
1,050	+42.0	11.5
1,100	+46.0	12.25

SCOPE ADJUSTMENT CHART IN MOA		
NOTES:		
CARTRIDGE: 7.62MM NATO (.308 WINCHESTER)		
BULLET: 168-GRAIN BOATTAIL HOLLOWPOINT		
VELOCITY: 2,700 FPS		
RANGE	**+ ELEV -**	**10 mph**
IN YARDS	**IN MINUTES**	**L WIND R**
100	0.0	.75
200	+2.0	1.5
300	+4.75	2.5
350	+6.5	3.0
400	+8.25	3.5
450	+10.0	4.0
500	+12.0	4.5
550	+14.25	5.0
600	+16.5	5.75
650	+18.75	6.25
700	+21.5	7.0
750	+24.25	7.75
800	+27.25	8.5
850	+30.5	9.25
900	+34.0	10.0
950	+37.75	10.75
1,000	+41.75	11.5

SCOPE ADJUSTMENT CHART IN MOA		
NOTES: M1A/M14 WITH SCOPE		
CARTRIDGE: 7.62MM NATO (.308 WINCHESTER)		
BULLET: 168-GRAIN BOATTAIL HOLLOWPOINT		
VELOCITY: 2,680 FPS		
RANGE	**+ ELEV -**	**10 mph**
IN YARDS	**IN MINUTES**	**L WIND R**
100	0.0	.75
200	+1.75	1.5
300	+4.5	2.5
350	+6.25	3.0
400	+8.0	3.5
450	+9.75	4.0
500	+11.75	4.5
550	+14.0	5.0
600	+16.0	5.5
650	+18.5	6.25
700	+21.0	6.75
750	+23.75	7.5
800	+26.75	8.0
850	+30.0	8.75
900	+33.25	9.5
950	+37.0	10.25
1,000	+40.75	11.0

SCOPE ADJUSTMENT CHART IN MOA		
NOTES:		
CARTRIDGE: 7.62MM NATO (.308 WINCHESTER)		
BULLET: 175-GRAIN BOATTAIL HOLLOWPOINT		
VELOCITY: 2,640 FPS		
RANGE	**+ ELEV -**	**10 mph**
IN YARDS	**IN MINUTES**	**L WIND R**
100	0.0	.75
200	+2.0	1.5
300	+5.0	2.25
350	+6.5	2.75
400	+8.5	3.0
450	+10.25	3.5
500	+12.25	4.0
550	+14.25	4.5
600	+16.5	5.0
650	+18.75	5.5
700	+21.25	6.25
750	+24.0	6.75
800	+26.75	7.25
850	+29.75	8.0
900	+33.0	8.5
950	+36.25	9.25

SCOPE ADJUSTMENT CHART IN MOA		
NOTES: CON'T FROM PAGE 139		
CARTRIDGE: 7.62MM NATO (.308 WINCHESTER)		
BULLET: 175-GRAIN BOATTAIL HOLLOWPOINT		
VELOCITY: 2,640 FPS		
RANGE	**+ ELEV -**	**10 mph**
IN YARDS	**IN MINUTES**	**L WIND R**
1,000	+39.75	10.0
1,050	+43.5	10.5
1,100	+47.75	11.25

SCOPE ADJUSTMENT CHART IN MOA		
NOTES:		
CARTRIDGE: .30-06 SPRINGFIELD		
BULLET: 168-GRAIN BOATTAIL HOLLOWPOINT		
VELOCITY: 2,800 FPS		
RANGE	**+ ELEV -**	**10 mph**
IN YARDS	**IN MINUTES**	**L WIND R**
100	0.0	.75
200	+1.75	1.5
300	+4.5	2.25
350	+6.0	2.75
400	+7.5	3.25
450	+9.25	3.75
500	+11.0	4.25
550	+13.0	4.75
600	+15.0	5.25
650	+17.25	6.0
700	+19.75	6.5
750	+22.25	7.25
800	+25.0	8.0
850	+28.0	8.5
900	+31.25	9.5
950	+34.5	10.25
1,000	+38.25	11.0

SCOPE ADJUSTMENT CHART IN MOA		
NOTES:		
CARTRIDGE: .30-06 SPRINGFIELD		
BULLET: 180-GRAIN BOATTAIL HOLLOWPOINT		
VELOCITY: 2,710 FPS		
RANGE	+ ELEV -	10 mph
IN YARDS	IN MINUTES	L WIND R
100	0.0	.75
200	+2.0	1.5
300	+4.75	2.25
350	+6.25	2.5
400	+7.75	3.0
450	+9.5	3.5
500	+11.5	4.0
550	+13.5	4.5
600	+15.5	5.0
650	+17.75	5.5
700	+20.0	6.0
750	+24.0	6.5
800	+25.25	7.0
850	+28.0	7.75
900	+31.0	8.25
950	+34.0	9.0

1,000	+37.5	9.5
1,050	+41.0	10.25
1,100	+44.75	11.0

SCOPE ADJUSTMENT CHART IN MOA		
NOTES:		
CARTRIDGE: .30-06 SPRINGFIELD		
BULLET: 200-GRAIN BOATTAIL HOLLOWPOINT		
VELOCITY: 2,500 FPS		
RANGE	**+ ELEV -**	**10 mph**
IN YARDS	**IN MINUTES**	**L WIND R**
100	0.0	.75
200	+2.5	1.5
300	+5.5	2.0
350	+7.25	2.5
400	+9.25	3.0
450	+11.25	3.5
500	+13.25	3.75
550	+15.5	4.25
600	+17.75	4.75
650	+20.25	5.25
700	+22.75	5.75
750	+25.5	6.25
800	+28.3	6.75
850	+31.25	7.25
900	+34.5	8.0
950	+37.75	8.5

1,000	+41.25	9.0
1,050	+45.0	9.5
1,100	+49.0	10.25

SCOPE ADJUSTMENT CHART IN MOA		
NOTES:		
CARTRIDGE: .300 WINCHESTER MAGNUM		
BULLET: 175-GRAIN BOATTAIL HOLLOWPOINT		
VELOCITY: 3,000 FPS		
RANGE	**+ ELEV -**	**10 mph**
IN YARDS	**IN MINUTES**	**L WIND R**
100	0.0	.5
200	+1.5	1.25
300	+3.5	1.75
350	+4.75	2.25
400	+6.0	2.5
450	+7.5	3.0
500	+9.0	3.5
550	+10.5	3.75
600	+12.25	4.25
650	+14.0	4.5
700	+15.75	5.0
750	+17.75	5.5
800	+19.75	6.0
850	+22.0	6.5
900	+24.25	7.0
950	+26.75	7.5

1,000	+29.25	8.25
1,050	+32.0	8.75
1,100	+35.0	9.5
1,150	+38.25	10.0
1,200	+41.5	10.5
1,250	+45.0	11.25
1,300	+49.0	12.0

SCOPE ADJUSTMENT CHART IN MOA		
NOTES:		
CARTRIDGE: .300 WINCHESTER MAGNUM		
BULLET: 190-GRAIN BOATTAIL HOLLOWPOINT		
VELOCITY: 2,900 FPS		
RANGE	**+ ELEV -**	**10 mph**
IN YARDS	**IN MINUTES**	**L WIND R**
100	0.0	.5
200	+1.25	1.25
300	+3.75	1.75
350	+5.25	.2.25
400	+6.5	2.5
450	+8.0	2.75
500	+9.5	3.25
550	+11.0	3.5
600	+12.75	4.0
650	+14.5	4.5
700	+16.5	5.0
750	+18.5	5.25
800	+20.5	5.75
850	+22.75	6.25
900	+25.25	6.75
950	+27.75	7.25

1,000	+30.25	7.75
1,050	+33.25	8.5
1,100	+36.0	9.0
1,150	+39.0	9.5
1,200	+42.5	10.25
1,250	+46.0	10.75
1,300	+49.75	11.25

SCOPE ADJUSTMENT CHART IN MOA		
NOTES:		
CARTRIDGE: .300 WINCHESTER MAGNUM		
BULLET: 220-GRAIN BOATTAIL HOLLOWPOINT		
VELOCITY: 2,700 FPS		
RANGE	+ ELEV -	10 mph
IN YARDS	IN MINUTES	L WIND R
100	0.0	0.5
200	+2.0	1.0
300	+4.5	1.75
350	+6.0	2.0
400	+7.5	2.25
450	+9.25	2.5
500	+11.0	3.0
550	+12.75	3.5
600	+14.5	3.75
650	+16.5	4.0
700	+18.5	4.5
750	+20.5	5.0
800	+23.0	5.5
850	+25.25	5.75
900	+27.75	6.0
950	+30.25	6.5
1,000	+33.0	7.0

1,050	+35.75	7.5
1,100	+38.75	8.0
1,150	+41.75	8.5
1,200	+45.0	9.0
1,250	+48.5	9.5
1,300	+52.25	10.25

SCOPE ADJUSTMENT CHART IN MOA		
NOTES:		
CARTRIDGE: .30-338		
BULLET: 180-GRAIN BOATTAIL HOLLOWPOINT		
VELOCITY: 3,500 FPS		
RANGE	+ ELEV -	10 mph
IN YARDS	IN MINUTES	L WIND R
100	0.0	.5
200	+.75	1.0
300	+2.25	1.5
350	+3.25	2.0
400	+4.25	2,25
450	+5.25	2.5
500	+6.25	2.75
550	+7.25	3.0
600	+8.5	3.25
650	+9.75	3.75
700	+11.0	4.0
750	+12.25	4.5
800	+13.75	5.0
850	+15.25	5.25
900	+17.0	5.5
950	+18.5	6.0
1,000	+20.5	6.5

1,050	+22.25	7.0
1,100	+24.5	7.5
1,150	+26.5	8.0
1,200	+28.75	8.5
1,250	+31.25	9.0
1,300	+33.75	9.5
1,350	+36.5	10.25
1,400	+39.5	10.75
1,450	+42.5	11.25
1,500	+45.75	12.0
1,550	+49.25	12.5
1,600	+53.0	13.25

SCOPE ADJUSTMENT CHART IN MOA		
NOTES:		
CARTRIDGE: .30-378 WEATHERBY MAGNUM		
BULLET: 200-GRAIN BOATTAIL HOLLOWPOINT		
VELOCITY: 3,500 FPS		
RANGE	+ ELEV -	10 mph
IN YARDS	IN MINUTES	L WIND R
100	0.0	.5
200	+.75	.75
300	+2.25	1.25
350	+3.0	1.5
400	+4.0	1.75
450	+5.0	2.0
500	+6.0	2,25
550	+7.0	2.5
600	+8.0	3.0
650	+9.25	3.25
700	+10.5	3.5
750	+11.5	3.75
800	+13.0	4.25
850	+14.5	4.5
900	+15.75	4.75
950	+17.25	5.0
1,000	+18.75	5.5

1,050	+20.5	6.0
1,100	+22.25	6.25
1,150	+24.0	6.5
1,200	+26.0	7.0
1,250	+28.0	7.5
1,300	+30.0	7.75
1,350	+32.5	8.25
1,400	+34.75	8.75
1,450	+37.25	9.25
1,500	+40.0	9.75
1,550	+42.75	10.25
1,600	+45.75	10.75
1,650	+49.0	11.25
1,700	+52.0	11.5
1,750	+55.75	12.5
1,800	+59.25	13.0

SCOPE ADJUSTMENT CHART IN MOA		
NOTES:		
CARTRIDGE: .303 BRITISH		
BULLET: 174-GRAIN BOATTAIL HOLLOWPOINT		
VELOCITY: 2,460 FPS		
RANGE	**+ ELEV -**	**10 mph**
IN YARDS	**IN MINUTES**	**L WIND R**
100	0.0	.75
200	+2.25	1.5
300	+5.5	2.5
350	+7.5	3.0
400	+9.5	3.5
450	+11.5	4.0
500	+14.0	4.5
550	+16.25	5.0
600	+19.0	5.5
650	+21.75	6.25
700	+24.5	6.75
750	+27.75	7.5
800	+31.25	8.25
850	+34.75	9.0
900	+38.75	9.5
950	+42.5	10.25
1,000	+46.5	11.0

SCOPE ADJUSTMENT CHART IN MOA		
NOTES:		
CARTRIDGE: 8MM X 57 MAUSER		
BULLET: 175-GRAIN SPITZER		
VELOCITY: 2,600 FPS		
RANGE	+ ELEV -	10 mph
IN YARDS	IN MINUTES	L WIND R
100	0.0	1.0
200	+2.25	2.0
300	+5.5	3.0
350	+7.5	3.75
400	+9.5	4.5
450	+11.75	5.0
500	+14.25	5.75
550	+16.75	6.5
600	+19.5	7.25
650	+22.5	8.25
700	+25.75	9.0
750	+29.5	10.0
800	+33.5	10.75
850	+37.5	11.75
900	+42.25	12.5
950	+47.0	13.5
1,000	+52.25	14.5

SCOPE ADJUSTMENT CHART IN MOA		
NOTES:		
CARTRIDGE: .338 WINCHESTER MAGNUM		
BULLET: 300-GRAIN BOATTAIL HOLLOWPOINT		
VELOCITY: 2,500 FPS		
RANGE	+ ELEV -	10 mph
IN YARDS	IN MINUTES	L WIND R
100	0.0	.75
200	+2.5	1.5
300	+5.5	2.25
350	+7.5	2.5
400	+9.25	3.0
450	+11.25	3.5
500	+13.5	4.0
550	+15.5	4.5
600	+18.0	4.75
650	+20.5	5.5
700	+23.0	6.0
750	+25.75	6.5
800	+28.5	7.0
850	+31.75	7.5
900	+35.0	8.25
950	+38.5	8.75

1,000	+42.0	9.25
1,050	+45.75	10.0
1,100	+50.0	10.5

SCOPE ADJUSTMENT CHART IN MOA		
NOTES: RIB MOUNTAIN ARMS MODEL 92		
BOLT-ACTION		
CARTRIDGE: .50 CALIBER BROWNING		
BULLET: 750-GRAIN BOATTAIL SPITZER		
VELOCITY: 2,750 FPS		
RANGE	**+ ELEV -**	**10 mph**
IN YARDS	**IN MINUTES**	**L WIND R**
100	0.0	.25
200	+1.25	.5
300	+3.5	1.0
350	+4.5	1.25
400	+6.0	1.5
450	+8.5	1.5
500	+10.0	1.75
550	+11.5	
600	+13.0	2.25
650	+14.5	
700	+16.25	2.5
750	+17.75	
800	+19.5	3.0
850	+21.25	
900	+23.0	3.25
950	+24.75	

1,000	+26.5	3.75
1,050	+28.5	
1,100	+30.5	4.25
1,150	+32.5	
1,200	+34.75	4.75
1,250	+36.75	
1,300	+39.0	5.25
1,350	+41.5	
1,400	+43.75	5.75
1,450	+46.25	
1,500	+48.5	6.25
1,550	+51.25	
1,600	+53.75	6.75
1,650	+56.5	
1,700	+59.5	7.5
1,750	+62.25	
1,800	+65.25	8.0
1,850	+68.25	
1,900	+71.5	8.5
2,000	+74.75	9.25

Appendix B

Long-Range Shooting Sources

The following are manufacturers, suppliers, and organizations that are sources of equipment or information for and about long-range shooting.

Bell & Carlson, Inc.
101 Allen Rd.
Dodge City Industrial Park
Dodge City, KS 67801

Bell & Carlson manufactures custom synthetic rifle stocks.

Berger Bullets
5342 West Camelback Rd. 200
Glendale, AZ 85301

Berger is a manufacturer of specialized low-drag and match bullets for competition and varminting.

Brownells, Inc.
200 South Front St.
Montezuma, IA 50171

Brownells is a one-stop catalog for most gunsmithing needs.

Burris, Inc.
Box 1747, Dept. 729
Greeley, CO 80632

This is a manufacturer of rifle scopes, mounts, and Posi-Align rings.

Bushnell
Bausch & Lomb
Sport Optic Division
9200 Cody
Overland Park, KS 66214

This is a manufacturer of rifle scopes, bore-sighting tools, and laser range finders.

Champions Choice
201 International Blvd.
LaVergne, TN 37086

This is a catalog for high-power and bull's-eye shooters that features Jim Owens' *Reading the Wind* and other books on high-power rifle shooting.

Dillon Precision Products, Inc.
7442 East Butherus Dr.
Scottsdale, AZ 85260

Dillon is a supplier of equipment for reloading (including automatic reloading presses) and all forms of shooting automatic reloading presses.

EKL Enterprises, Inc.
5465 Pine Rd.
Black Earth, WI 53515

EKL is a company owned by Earl Liebetrau, who is a two-time winner of the Wimbledon Cup 1,000-Yard Championship. It builds custom long-range competition rifles and adjustable spotting scope stands.

Hodgdon Powder Company
P.O. Box 2932, Dept. VH497
Shawnee Mission, KS 66201

This company sells an extensive line of gunpowders for all types of shooting.

Hornady Mfg. Co.
Box 1848
Grand Island, NE 68802

This outfit manufactures production bullets. The A Max line of bullets is its low-drag design and includes its 750-grain .50-caliber for the BMG cartridge.

H-S Precision
1301 Turbine Dr.
Rapid City, SD 57701

H-S Precision produces custom long-range rifles and synthetic rifle stocks.

Leica Camera, Inc.
156 Ludlow Ave.
Northvale, NJ 07647

Leica manufactures Geovid laser range finders, binoculars, and spotting scopes.

Midway
5875 West Van Horn Tavern Rd.
Dept. D
Columbia, MO 65203

This is a retail shooters' supply and offers just about everything you'll need to go shooting.

Flint & Frizzen Gun Shop
8735 Dixie Highway
Clarkston, MI 48348

Bruce McArthur makes the best muzzle brakes we have ever used. They work exceptionally well and have no adverse effect on accuracy. They are capable of reducing the felt recoil of an 18-pound .50-caliber BMG rifle to that of a 12-gauge slug gun. They are available for a wide range of uses.

National Rifle Association (NRA)
11250 Waples Mill Rd.
Fairfax, VA 22030-9400

If you aren't a member, join.

Nosler, Inc.
P.O. Box 671
Bend, OR 97709

Nosler is a manufacturer of production bullets, including varmint and other types of hunting bullets.

Oehler Research, Inc.
P.O. Box 9135
Austin, TX 78766

Oehler makes high-quality chronographs and ballistic software.

Redfield, Inc.
5800 East Jewell Ave.
Denver, CO 80224

Redfield is a manufacturer of rifle scopes, spotting scopes, and bore-sighting tools.

Rib Mountain Arms
P.O. Box 8
Sturgis, SD 57785

Manufacturer of superaccurate long-range rifles. Their Model 92 is a single-shot, bolt-action .50-caliber BMG capable of 2,000-yard-plus accuracy. Its Model 95 bolt-action is designed for the .30-378 and is capable of 1,800-yard accuracy and it doesn't leave the shop until it's right.

Sierra Bullets
1400 West Henry St.
Sedalia, MO 65301

Sierra is a major player in commercial low-drag match bullets. Their Sierra III software package is an easy-to-use ballistic program that plots trajectories for all ranges and conditions.

Sinclair International
2330 Wayne Haven St.
Fort Wayne, IN 46803

Sinclair is a source of supplies and equipment for precision shooting.

Tar-Hunt Custom Rifles
RR 3, Box 572
Bloomsburg, PA 17815

These guys have been building high-grade bench-rest, varmint, and sporter rifles since 1981. They were also the first to produce a bolt-action slug rifle. Their design is still the state of the art that all slug guns are measured against.

Timber Beast Products (TBP), Inc.
P.O. Box 67
Eureka, WI 54934
Tel. (920) 987-5052

Without a doubt, TBP makes the best long-range bullets in the world. Of course, I (Warren) may be biased, since I own the company. I make rebated boattail low-drag bullets in .224 Weatherby Magnum, .243 Winchester, and .308

Winchester calibers. I offer speciality items such as fragmenting cores and custom weights for varminters, plus precision flat-based bench-rest bullets.

Unertl
P.O. Box 818
Mars, PA 16046-0818

Unertl manufactures fine external adjustment scopes and supplies the U.S. Marines with an interal adjustment model. It supplies scope blocks and repair services on its older scopes.

Weaver
A Division of Blount, Inc.
P.O. Box 856
Lewiston, ID 83501

Weaver makes high-quality long-range scopes that won't break the bank. Its V16, V24, and KT15 scopes offer good magnification and accurate adjustments at a very reasonable price.

About the Authors

Warren Gabrilska is a manufacturing/finishing engineer, author, and entrepreneur whose major passion is shooting. He is an NRA-certified rifle and pistol instructor who holds sharpshooter classifications in ISU smallbore and air rifle and an expert classification in NRA high-power rifle competition. He competes in IPSC pistol and three-gun matches and Second Chance bowling pin competitions. Warren is the owner of Timber Beast Products, Inc., which makes custom long-range low-drag bullets for competitive shooters, hunters, and varminters.

Tony M. Noblitt is an operating engineer and jack of all trades. He is an avid varmint and big-game hunter, bullet designer, experimental shooter, and reloader. Tony has shot in NBRSA bench-rest matches, as well as trap, skeet, and sporting clays competitions. He was driven to write this book after finding that this type of material wasn't available when he first decided to go long range. He has the enviable privilege of having a 1,000-yard range right off his back patio. The ability to step out the patio door to the shooting bench and shoot on a whim has given him a great deal of practical experience shooting long range.

Both Warren and Tony are long-time voting members of the NRA.